The Evolution of China's Diplomacy in the Modern Era

Edited by Yang Jiemian

Published by
ACA Publishing Ltd.
University House
11-13 Lower Grosvenor Place,
London SW1W 0EX, UK
Tel: +44 (0)20 7834 7676 Fax: +44 (0)20 7973 0076
E-mail: info@alaincharlesasia.com

Web: www.alaincharlesasia.com
Beijing Office
Tel:+86(0)10 8472 1250 Fax:86(0)10 5885 0639
Written by Yang Jiemian
Edited by Martin Savery
Translated by Sun Xinwei
© People's Publishing House, 2015
This translation is published by ACA Publishing Ltd in association with People's Publishing House

ALL RIGHTS RESERVED. NO PART OF THIS
PUBLICATION MAY BE REPRODUCED IN MATERIAL FORM,
BY ANY MEANS, WHETHER GRAPHIC,
ELECTRONIC, MECHANICAL OR OTHER, INCLUDING
PHOTOCOPYING OR INFORMATION STORAGE, IN
WHOLE OR IN PART, AND MAY NOT BE USED TO PREPARE
OTHER PUBLICATIONS WITHOUT WRITTEN
PERMISSION FROM THE PUBLISHER.

The greatest care has been taken to ensure accuracy but the publisher can accept no responsibility for errors or omissions, or for any liability occasioned by relying on its content.
ISBN 978-1-910760-12-3
The Evolution of China's Diplomacy in the Modern Era is available from the National Bibliographic Service of the British Library.

Preface

What is the state system of China? How has the Communist Party of China (CPC) managed to exercize long-term governance and to lead the Chinese people from one victory to another? What are the 'secrets' of the CPC's governance? What is China's development road? What significant strategies have been adopted in China? What is the next step in China's development? Why has China been able to achieve such rapid economic development? These are just some of the many questions frequently asked by the international community, especially foreign political parties and statesmen on their visits to China. For the purpose of providing answers to these questions and enabling readers to be informed about the real China and the CPC, we arranged for the *Understanding Modern China* Series (hereinafter referred to as the Series) to be written, to serve as elementary documents introducing the CPC, as well as China's development road, development theories and development experience.

The Series is inspired by the new philosophies, new ideas and new strategies for the country's governance put forward by General Secretary Xi Jinping since the 18th National Congress of the CPC, aimed at the following aspects: strenuously reflecting the development vision of 'the Chinese Dream' and the development prospects of the 'Two Centenary' goals; strenuously reflecting the coordinated promotion of the overall situation of a 'five-pronged approach to building socialism with Chinese characteristics to build up socialist economy, socialist democracy, socialist advanced culture, socialist harmonious society and socialist ecological civilisation; and the strategic arrangements for the 'Four-Pronged Comprehensive Strategy' comprehensively completing the building of a moderately prosperous society in all respects, comprehensively deepening reform in all respects, comprehensively advancing the rule of law, and comprehensively exercising strict discipline for the party; strenuously reflecting the 'new normal' facilitating and leading China's economic development and the implementation of the 'five major development concepts' to promote innovative, coordinated, green, open and shared development; strenuously reflecting the three major economic development strategies of the 'Belt and Road', the coordinated development of Beijing, Tianjin and Hebei province, and the Yangtze river economic belt. On the basis of a great number of fresh cases and experiences, the Series tells China's story, transmits China's voice, analyzes China's problems, and offers China solutions.

The Series has been written on the basis of telling China's story and transmitting China's voice, oriented around the following four aspects: the first is to illustrate the new measures taken to deepen reform since the 18th National Congress of the CPC, the new ideas on economic development and the new philosophy on foreign affairs, on the basis of an all-round introduction to the achievements since the reform and opening up; the second is to analyze the reason for the achievements, the underlying operating law, and the process of evolution, while presenting the development achievements of China's economy and society; the third is to keep to problem orientation and demand orientation, rather than attempt to be all-embracing and systematic, so as to clear up targeted doubts and confusion on the basis of the demands of foreign readers; the fourth is to introduce China not only in terms of 'where it is coming from', but also in terms of 'where it is going', for the purpose of enabling readers to know about China's historical development process on the one hand, and on the other hand, exemplifying and clarifying how China assures the organic unification of its past, present and future, the organic combination of legacy and innovation, and how China is planning its future development.

Under the guidance of the International Department of the CPC Central Committee, the writing of the Series has been organized by China Executive Leadership Academy Pudong (CELAP).

The International Department of the CPC Central Committee is the functional department of the CPC in charge of foreign affairs. So far, the CPC has established connections of various types with more than 600 political parties and organizations in over 160 countries and regions, which include left-wing and right-wing parties; both ruling parties and opposition parties. Foreign affairs work is of paramount importance to the CPC, and an indispensable component of national diplomacy as a whole, whose target is to promote state-to-state and people-to-people communication and understanding.

Preface

CELAP is a national leadership institution in China, and as a platform on which international cooperative training and exchange are carried out, CELAP has held fast to its characteristics of internationality and openness since March 2005 when it was founded. CELAP spares no effort in implementing international cooperative training, with target participants being foreign political parties and statesmen, high-ranking business executives and senior professionals. By the end of 2015, CELAP had offered training programs to more than 6,000 participants from over 130 countries, and thus has won wide recognition and received a favorable reception from the countries, regions and participants that are involved.

To cater for the needs of foreign participants, CELAP initiated the writing of the Series at the beginning of 2012, and after four years of modifications and improvements, the finalized manuscripts were completed at the end of 2015. The first batch of 10 books to be published in this Series are: *China's New Strategies for Governing the Country*; *The Communist Party of China: the Past, Present and Future of Party Building*; *China's Reform, Opening Up and Construction of Development Zones*; *The Framework of the Chinese Government and Public Services*; *A New Analysis of Urbanization in China*; *China's Agriculture and Rural Development in the Post-Reform Era*; *The Evolution of China's Diplomacy in the Modern Era*; *Leadership Selection and Appointment in China*; *Leadership Education and Training in China*; and *Shanghai – the 'Pacesetter' of China's Reform and Opening Up*.

The authors of the Series are mainly professionals in CELAP, and functionaries and specialists in the Development Research Center of the Shanghai Municipal People's Government, Shanghai Institute for International Studies and Hangzhou Research Center for Urban Studies.

The Series is published in Chinese and English, with the English translation done mainly by senior professors at Shanghai International Studies University, to whom thanks are due. Gratitude also goes to the People's Publishing House for its great support and positive suggestions in the process of writing and translating.

Writing such a series of textbooks for mature foreign students is a first in China. Constructive criticism is welcome, for the Series as a new endeavor can hardly be free from mistakes.

Editorial Committee of the *Understanding Modern China* Series
January 2016

The Editorial Committee of the Understanding Modern China Series

Directors: Guo Yezhou Feng Jun

Vice Directors: Zhou Zhongfei   An Yuejun

Members: (Listed alphabetically)

An Yuejun	Chen Zhong	Feng Jun
Guo Yezhou	He Lisheng	Jiang Haishan
Li Man	Li Yanhui	Liu Genfa
Liu Jingbei	Wang Guoping	Wang Jinding
Yang Jiemian	Zhao Shiming	Zheng Jinzhou
Zhou Zhenhua	Zhou Zhongfei	

Editor-in-Chief: Feng Jun

Alain Charles Asia (ACA) Publishing Ltd is delighted to be associated with the People's Publishing House to bring this series of 10 *Understanding Modern China* books to an English-speaking readership.

ACA, formerly known as ACP (Alain Charles Publishing) Ltd Beijing, was founded in October 1989 and was the first foreign-owned publishing company to be allowed to open an office in China.

In 2007, ACP Beijing was renamed ACA Publishing Ltd to better reflect its focus on China and the Asia-Pacific region. The company specialises in publishing books about China for international readers and has offices in Beijing and London.

ACA Publishing Ltd,

February 2019

Contents

Introduction X
    I. Objectives and Expectations....................................... XII
    II. Structure of the Book XIII
    III. Key Points and Difficulties XIV
    IV. Requirements XV

1. The Concepts and Strategies of China's Diplomacy.................. 1
    I. Principal Concepts of China's Diplomacy 1
    II. Main Strategies of China's Diplomacy 8

2. China's Relations with Neighboring Countries............................ 15
    I. The Formation and Evolution of China's Good-Neighborly Diplomatic Ideology 16
    II. China's Economic Relations with Neighboring Countries 19
    III. China's Political Relations with Neighboring Countries 23
    IV. China's Security Relationship with Peripheral Countries........ 33

3. The Development of China's Diplomacy with Big Countries.... 40
    I. Changes in China's Diplomacy with Big Countries................ 41
    II. The Development of China's Diplomacy with Emerging Powers (BRICS) 54

4. China's Diplomacy with Other Developing Countries............. 66
    I. Principal Concepts of China's Diplomacy with Other Developing Countries... 66
    II. China's Contribution to South-South Cooperation................ 70
    III. New Progress in China-Africa Relations 76

5. China's Practice in Multilateral Diplomacy 86
   I. Reasons Why China is an Active Advocate and Practitioner of Multilateral Diplomacy 86
   II. The UN is an Important Platform for China's Multilateral Diplomacy 93
   III. China is an Important Participant in the Reform of Global Economic Governance Mechanisms 99
   IV. China is an Active Participant in Addressing Global Climate Change 104

6. How China Conducts Public Diplomacy 110
   I. Reasons for China to Carry out Public Diplomacy During Recent Years 110
   II. The Principles Underpinning China's Development of Public Diplomacy 115
   III. New Practices and Characteristics of China's Public Diplomacy 118
   IV. Challenges of China's Public Diplomacy 124

Chapter Follow-up Questions and References 128

Introduction

Since the founding of the People's Republic of China (PRC) 70 years ago, and, more specifically, since the reform and opening up more than 40 years ago, China's diplomacy with the rest of the world has undergone historic changes due to a dramatic and comprehensive growth in its national strength, a quick rise in its international status, and an enormous increase in its global influence. As it is playing an increasingly significant role in regional and international affairs, China has become the focus of global attention. 'China fever' is gaining momentum worldwide.

While China's rapidly growing economy has brought huge opportunities for the world's economic development, China has also brought positive energy to the management of international affairs. In doing so, it has gained widespread recognition and acclaim from the international community. All of these achievements have been a result of China being rapidly ushered onto the center of the world stage. Talk of 'China as a land of opportunity' and 'China's contribution to the world economy' is prevalent in the international community. Since its reform and opening up, China has increasingly involved itself in economic globalization and for the past 40 years has maintained an economic growth rate of some 10% annually. China is ranked as the world's second largest economy. Even when faced with the global financial crisis China still managed to grow at 9% annually. The international community holds an increasingly firm belief that China will become the largest economy in the foreseeable future. As the largest and fastest emerging market, China is at the top of the rapidly growing nations and serves as a major and important driving force in enhancing globalization and the expansion of world trade. China's development promotes global development, and global development is inseparable from China. In addition, with its extensive participation in international affairs while positioning itself at the center of the world stage,

Introduction

China is playing an increasingly crucial role in upholding global peace and stability, and facilitating international cooperation and global governance.

On the other hand, China's rapid development has brought about a major transformation of the international system. Since the beginning of the modern era this is the first time that a non-Western country has rapidly risen up, causing Western nations to become suspicious of this transition of power. Over the past decade there have been three topics which have emerged regarding China: that 'China poses a threat to the world'; that 'China has become more aggressive' and that 'China's future is uncertain'. The argument that 'China poses a threat' to the world suggests that China's rising power will lead it to follow the path of modern Western countries and that, in turn, it will become a 'revolutionist' and 'revisionist' power destabilizing international order. The argument that China is becoming more aggressive exaggerates China's rapid growth, suggesting that it will become increasingly aggressive in terms of its diplomacy and eager to demonstrate its power in international and regional affairs. The argument that China's future is uncertain concedes that China is currently following a path of peaceful development. It argues that a myriad of uncertainties exist in China's future development and diplomatic strategies. All of these arguments reflect the concerns of the international community regarding China's future development.

Meanwhile, the international community has increased its expectations of China. In recent years there has been much discussion regarding 'China's responsibility', and this has become a hot topic. This debate particularly intensified during the global financial crisis. An accelerated transition of international power was the main impact of the global financial crisis on Western nations, causing more global issues to emerge. This in turn resulted in a juxtaposition between an increased demand for international commodities and a lack of supply. Against the backdrop of global crisis, Western countries that were the former suppliers of international public products have started to concentrate on dealing with their domestic economic and social problems. Thus their capability and willingness to supply public products to meet international market demand has decreased sharply. The international community expects much from China due to the dramatic rise of its national strength and international status. All developed and developing countries require or hope that China will become more actively involved in international affairs by shouldering more international responsibilities and obligations. China's responsibilities cover a wide range of areas, from economic balance, human rights, democracy, values, security issues, and regional hotspots, as well as global governance issues such as energy, environmental protection and foreign aid. China is expected to play a more important role and to become 'a responsible major power' which can supply more public products to the international community.

The speculation and contrasting views mentioned above can be summarized as follows: What kind of development path does China choose? What does China's development mean to the world? What ideas and theories guide China's diplomacy? What diplomatic policies does China pursue? How will China's rise impact neighboring countries? Will China break away from the traditional pattern of 'a rising power always seeking hegemony'? Will developing countries benefit from China's development? How does China define its international role and its participation in multilateral governance? How does China conduct public diplomacy? All of these questions demonstrate the world's desire to learn more about China's diplomatic thinking, beliefs and practice, and to share the experience of China's peaceful development.

This book aims to answer all of these questions so as to comprehensively, objectively and realistically address the world's eagerness to know about the beliefs, practices and experiences underlying China's peaceful development of diplomacy, and to improve the international community's knowledge and understanding of it.

I. Objectives and Expectations

This book begins with the fundamental principles of the peaceful development of China's diplomacy. It focuses on the policies and practices since the founding of the People's Republic of China (PRC), especially since the reform and opening up and since the start of the 21st century. This book seeks to answer the questions that concern the international community and foreign students. It is written in detailed and clear language, providing a panoramic view of the rich content and fundamental features of China's path of peaceful development and peaceful diplomatic policies. It will help readers to accurately comprehend internal and external conditions, as well as the major diplomatic tasks that China faces. This book also aims at helping readers to acquire an accurate and comprehensive knowledge of China's diplomatic guidelines, strategic deployments and policy implementation in dealing with global, regional and territorial issues. It also explains China's plan for future development so that the international community and foreign students will gain a full and objective understanding of China's diplomacy and peaceful development.

II. Structure of the Book

This book consists of six chapters. The first chapter provides an overview of the principles and strategies of China's diplomacy to enhance international as well as regional peace, development, cooperation and mutual advantage while endeavoring to maintain and promote national interests and to facilitate the construction of a community with a shared future for humanity. China's diplomatic strategies include global, regional, national and territorial strategies. China's commitment to peaceful development is the fundamental approach to the realization of its diplomatic strategies and is determined by multiple factors such as the tradition, values, interests and implementation of China's diplomacy.

The focus of the second chapter is China's diplomatic relations with neighboring countries. China's diplomatic relations with its neighboring countries play a vital role and are given top priority in China's development and diplomacy. The chapter discusses this good-neighborly diplomacy from various perspectives, for example, the strategic thinking of China's diplomatic relations with its neighbors and the peripheral economic, political and security situations.

The third chapter focuses on the development of China's diplomatic relations with developed countries. It emphasizes the strategic thinking behind China's exploration of new types of relations with developed countries and the diplomatic practice of setting up a general and dynamically-balanced network of relations with major powers. It introduces China's foreign strategic role, its major tasks, and its current development situation. It also introduces the three-tiered position, key tasks, development status and prospects of China's major diplomatic strategy with traditional Western powers such as the United States, emerging powers including the BRICS (Brazil, Russia, China, India and South Africa), and major regional powers so as to push ahead for mutually beneficial cooperation between China and the major world powers.

The fourth chapter details China's diplomatic relations with developing countries. It highlights the fact that building its relationships with developing countries forms the very foundation of China's diplomacy, and that strengthening such development is a key point in the whole process of promoting China's diplomatic relations with developing countries. The chapter introduces new Chinese concepts such as common development, shared development and the co-establishment of diplomatic mechanisms with developing countries.

The fifth chapter elaborates on China's multilateral diplomacy. It introduces the historical changes in China's diplomatic relations with the rest of the world since reform and opening up. It also discusses consequent major changes in China's beliefs, role, actions and interests in the international system. The chapter also discusses topics such as how China conducts multilateral diplomacy within the United Nations (UN), how China is engaged in the reform of the global governance mechanism and how China deals with global climate change, so as to make it clear that China plays an important role in building and contributing to multilateral diplomatic practices.

The sixth chapter discusses China's public diplomacy, primarily by introducing internal and external driving forces, new concepts, major practices, and the challenges facing China when it conducts its public diplomacy in the new era. It also provides the world with an authentic view of China. The purpose of China's public diplomacy is to strengthen exchanges and communication with other societies and nations. By extension it will enhance China's image, improve foreign public attitudes towards China and increase understanding, trust and cooperation between China and the rest of the world.

III. Key Points and Difficulties

The main focus of the book is its comprehensive introduction of the diplomatic policies and practices of China's peaceful development. Helping foreign students to understand that China's unwavering commitment to peaceful development is an inevitable choice to maintain China's national situation, socialist system, historical aspects, cultural traditions, and the protection of its own interests. This book also elaborates upon China's concept of innovation and practical experience in conducting diplomatic relations with neighboring countries, major countries and developing countries, and in carrying out multilateral and public diplomacy. This will enable the international community to acquire a comprehensive understanding of the history, current situation, and future development of China's peaceful diplomacy.

The challenges of writing the book lie in how to present China's diplomatic issues of common interest to foreign students in precise yet plain language. These issues should not only embody Chinese characteristics but also summarize the Chinese experience for universal use. The difficulties of the book also lie in how to provide foreign students with practical and useful teaching material so that they can understand the further meaning and implications of what they are learning, and apply what they have learned.

IV. Requirements

This book is flexible and open to change and adaptation. It provides fundamental background knowledge and a developmental outline of China's modern diplomacy, however it fails to portray the whole picture of the groundbreaking development of China's diplomacy. Teachers should update their course contents with new concepts and practices of China's diplomatic development to meet students' differing interests and needs. Teachers should also supplement their courses with various aids such as pictures, case studies, photos and charts to present China's diplomatic achievements in a more direct way.

It's quite likely that this book is not totally free from some flaws and mistakes due to limitations of the authors' knowledge and experience. Therefore, comments are welcome. The authors of this textbook are Yang Jiemian (Chapter 1), Chen Dongxiao (Chapter 3), Yu Xintian (Chapter 6), Cai Penghong (Chapter 2), Zhang Haibing (Chapter 4) and Zhang Pei (Chapter 5).

Chapter 1

The Concepts and Strategies of China's Diplomacy

Diplomatic thinking, perspectives and viewpoints are collectively referred to as diplomatic concepts. Diplomatic strategy, the long-term and holistic diplomatic planning, mainly involves strategic objectives, approaches, conditions and constraints. The core of China's diplomatic concepts and strategy is to maintain and advance national interests and build a community with a shared future for humanity as well as to uphold peace, promote development and pursue cooperation and mutual benefit at both international and regional levels.

I. Principal Concepts of China's Diplomacy

In its white paper entitled *China's Peaceful Development Path* which was released in December 2005, the Chinese government explicitly stated that 'peace, opening up, cooperation, harmony and mutually beneficial policies remain our position, philosophy, doctrine, and pursuit'. At the 18th National Congress of the CPC held in November 2012, the Chinese government reiterated that 'China will unswervingly commit itself to the path of peaceful development and uphold independent and peaceful diplomatic policies'.

1) The Five Principles of Peaceful Co-existence

The 20th century marked the most humiliating and war-stricken period in Chinese history. Chinese pioneers endured untold hardships and made painstaking efforts in seeking approaches to rejuvenate and empower the nation. Under the leadership of the CPC the Chinese people ultimately achieved a final victory and founded the People's Republic of China (PRC) after continuous fighting from 1921 to 1949.

When the PRC was founded, it needed to establish and develop friendly and cooperative relations with all other peace-loving nations so as to create a favorable international environment with neighboring countries as well as countries from afar. In celebrating the founding of the PRC on October 1, 1949, Chairman Mao Zedong made a solemn announcement to the world that "our government is the only legal government of the Chinese people and we are ready to establish diplomatic relations with any foreign governments willing to abide by the principles of equality, mutual benefit and respect for territorial sovereignty".

In 1954, China, together with India and Burma (modern-day Myanmar), issued a joint communiqué known as the 'Five Principles of Peaceful Co-existence', characterized by 'respecting sovereignty and territorial integrity, non-aggression and non-interference in the domestic affairs of other countries, thereby achieving mutual benefit on the basis of equality and peaceful co-existence'.

China has adhered to the 'Five Principles' in developing its diplomatic relations with other countries and has written it into the 1975, 1978 and 1982 (current) versions of the *Constitution of the PRC*. So far, more than 100 bilateral agreements have been signed between the Chinese government and foreign governments and all have adhered to the 'Five Principles'. Acting on the basis of the 'Five Principles', China has actively developed diplomatic relations with other nations with different social systems. By July 31, 2011, the number of countries which had established diplomatic relations with China had risen to 172.

2) The Concepts of Peaceful Development, a Harmonious World and a Community with a Shared Future for Humanity

The entire concept of China's peaceful development has been gradually formulated and developed since the late 1980s, and the concept of world harmony was put forward in 2005. Both of these are the guidelines of China's diplomacy.

(1) The Concept of Peaceful Development

In 1983, Deng Xiaoping, the core of the second generation of the Chinese collective leadership, made the strategic judgment that it was unlikely that a new world war would occur. In 1985, he elaborated his main ideas of the era – that "the really important and strategic issues facing the whole world are peace, the economy and development".[1] By the mid-1980s, Deng Xiaoping had essentially developed the concept of 'peace and development' as a

---

[1] Deng Xiaoping *Deng Xiaoping's Selected Works*. Beijing: People's Publishing House, 1993. Vol.3, pages 25 & 105

replacement of the old 'war and revolution', and this concept has served to guide China's reform and opening up ever since

China's concept of peaceful development is based on the general judgment of the global political, economic, security and social situations. It deems that countries have become increasingly interdependent in the context of globalization. They have maintained world peace for seven decades since the end of the Second World War, and have made significant progress in economic and social development. Through building appropriate mechanisms, countries have increasingly reached consensus, thereby safeguarding and enhancing world peace, development and mutually beneficial cooperation.

In December 2005, the Chinese government released its white paper entitled *China's Peaceful Development Path*, which practically and theoretically summarized the process of China's peaceful development. In September 2011, in accordance with the prevailing situation, China released another white paper entitled *China's Peaceful Development*, which initially proposed actively fulfilling its international responsibility and added the notion of ecological environment protection and an official definition of China's core interests to the harmonious world concept. The core interests include national sovereignty, territorial integrity, national unification, the political state system and overall social stability, and the basic safeguards for ensuring sustainable economic and social development. All of this provides a practical approach to the realization of new security concepts such as mutual trust, mutual benefit and equality. It also enhances coordination in the three aspects of comprehensive security, common security, and cooperative security.

New Concepts of Security

China's new security concepts, initiated at the ASEAN Forum in 1995, have been constantly enriched and developed further, constituting the core of China's diplomatic strategy. On July 31, 2002 the Chinese delegation attending the foreign ministers' meeting of the ASEAN Forum presented the Document of China's Stand on New Security Concepts. This document elaborated upon new security concepts focusing on 'mutual trust, mutual benefit, equality, and coordination'. The white paper entitled China's Peaceful Development released by the Chinese government in September 2011 pointed out that China advocated these new security concepts 'in the hope of seeking comprehensive security, common security, and cooperative security'.

> On May 21, 2014, Chinese President Xi Jinping delivered a keynote speech at the 4th Summit of the Conference on Interaction and Confidence Building Measures in Asia (CICA) held in Shanghai. In his speech, President Xi proposed to actively advocate a concept of "a common, comprehensive, cooperative, sustainable security and create new security concepts". 'Common' means that the security of every country should be respected and guaranteed. 'Cooperative' suggests that all countries should promote internal and regional security through dialogue and cooperation. 'Sustainable' indicates that all countries should focus on both development and security to achieve sustainable and durable security.

(2) The Harmonious World Concept

The idea of 'building a socialist harmonious society' was initially put forward in *The Decision of the CPC Central Committee on Strengthening Governing Abilities* and was approved at the Fourth Plenary Session of the 16th Party Congress in September 2004. In April 2005, former President Hu Jintao initially proposed the concept of a "harmonious world" to the international community when attending activities in commemoration of the 50th Anniversary of the Bandung Conference. In September of the same year, Hu Jintao further elaborated this concept in the conference marking the 60th anniversary of the UN, laying a foundation for China's view on a "harmonious world". The theories of building a harmonious society internally and promoting a harmonious world externally have up to now been the guidelines for China's domestic and diplomatic affairs in the modern era.

The Harmonious World Concept

> On September 15, 2005, former President Hu Jintao delivered a speech entitled *Striving to Build a Harmonious World of Enduring Peace and Common Prosperity* in a summit meeting to celebrate the 60th anniversary of the founding of the UN. In the speech, he gave a detailed elaboration of 'building a harmonious world', which included the main ideas of adhering to multilateralism in seeking common security, adhering to mutually beneficial cooperation in seeking common prosperity, upholding the spirit of tolerance in seeking joint efforts to build a harmonious world, and adopting active and careful approaches in seeking the advance of UN reforms. In its white paper entitled *China's Peaceful Development* released in September 2011 the Chinese government further explained that 'politically, all countries should respect each other and treat each other as equals, and work together to

promote democracy in international relations'. 'Economically, all countries should cooperate with each other, draw on each other's strengths and make economic globalization a balanced and mutually beneficial process'. 'Culturally, all countries should learn from each other, seek common ground while putting aside differences, and respect the diversity of the world so as to promote the progress and prosperity of human civilization'. 'In terms of security, all countries should trust each other, strengthen cooperation and settle international disputes peacefully rather than resorting to war so as to jointly safeguard world peace and stability'. 'With regard to environmental protection, all countries should help each other and make a concerted effort to protect our only home... the planet Earth'.

The concept of building a harmonious world gradually formed and developed under multiple forces in the 60-year history since the founding of the PRC, which marked a significant milestone in the general principles of China's diplomacy. The harmonious world concept can be traced back very far into China's past. Confucius and Mencius respectively developed the concepts of 'a gentleman gets along with others, but does not necessarily agree with them while an unkind person agrees with others, but does not get along with them', and 'opportunities vouchsafed by heaven are less important than earthly advantages, which in turn are less important than unity among people'. Taoism, another major school of thought in ancient China, promoted the idea of harmonious coexistence between people and nature. This means that people should coexist harmoniously with nature, seeking the opportunity to survive and to develop while respecting and preserving it. Since the Qin and Han dynasties, the concept of a harmonious existence being universally applied has been embedded into the thoughts of various schools at various times. Thus it developed into a widely accepted humanitarian spirit in traditional Chinese philosophy and culture.

The concept of building a harmonious world caters to a growing historical trend. It regards the world as an integrated whole and focuses on building a world of durable peace and prosperity throughout all countries, politically, respecting each other and treating each other as equals, and working together to promote democracy in international relations; economically, cooperating with each other, drawing on each other's strengths and making economic globalization a balanced and win-win process that benefits all countries; culturally, learning from each other and seeking common ground while putting aside differences, respecting the diversity of the world, and promoting progress in human civilization; in terms of security, trusting each other and strengthening cooperation, settling international disputes and conflicts peacefully rather than resorting to war, and jointly safeguarding world peace and stability; and in terms of environmental protection, helping each other and making concerted efforts to better protect our only home — the Earth. The concept of building a harmonious world elaborates China's vision and proposal about the prospect of world development, and provides the international community with an international public product.

3) The Concept of a Community with a Shared Future for humanity

In November 2012, the idea of 'a community with a shared future for humanity' first appeared in a report to the 18th National Congress of the CPC. The report stated that win-win cooperation needed the awareness of a community with a shared future for humanity, which expected countries to stick together in times of difficulty, share rights and shoulder obligations, and boost the common interests of mankind. Since then, Chinese President Xi Jinping has repeatedly emphasized heightening the awareness on a series of important bilateral and multilateral diplomatic occasions. He has proposed building a China-ASEAN community of shared destiny, a China-Pakistan community of shared destiny, an Asian community of shared destiny, a China-Latin American and Caribbean Countries community of shared destiny, and a community of shared destiny with African countries. In September 2015, Xi Jinping made an important speech entitled *Working Together to Forge a New Partnership of Win-Win Cooperation and Create a Community with a Shared Future for Humanity* at the General Debate of the 70th Session of the UN General Assembly at the UN Headquarters in New York. In January 2017, Xi Jinping delivered a keynote speech entitled *Working Together to Build a Community with a Shared Future for Humanity* at the UN Headquarters in Geneva. In this speech, he elaborated on the concept of how to build a community with a shared future for humanity, giving answers to the questions on what had happened to the world and how we should respond. In October 2017, Xi Jinping, General Secretary of the CPC Central Committee, explicitly stated that to build a community with a shared future for humanity is the lofty goal of China's diplomacy, and called on the people of all countries to work together to "build an open, inclusive, clean and beautiful world that enjoys lasting peace, universal security, and common prosperity."

The concept of a community with a shared future for humanity is a proactive approach to the developmental trend of human society, based on the insights into the international situation and general changing trends of the world pattern. It reflects a global vision beyond narrow-minded national and state interests, state-to-state relationships, and differences in ideologies. It's how China ponders over the future of mankind. Ideally, the international community should endeavor to achieve 'a community with a shared future for humanity' that isn't just an abstract, imaginary concept. The Chinese government has continuously deepened and elaborated it into specific targets that can be phased in gradually.

> **The Concept of a Community with a Shared Future for Humanity**
>
> *In November 2012, the report to the 18th National Congress of the CPC proposed, for the first time, the idea of a community with a shared future for humanity and advocated to establish its awareness to boost the common interests of mankind. On September 28, 2015, Xi Jinping made an important speech entitled Working Together to Forge a New Partnership of Win-Win Cooperation and to Create a Community with a Shared Future for Humanity at the General Debate of the 70th Session of the UN General Assembly at the UN Headquarters in New York. In the speech, Xi stressed that the international community should build partnerships in which countries treat each other as equals, engage in mutual consultation and show mutual understanding; create a security architecture featuring fairness, justice, joint contribution and shared benefits; increase inter-civilization exchanges to promote harmony, inclusiveness and respect for differences; and build an ecosystem that puts mother nature and green development first. On January 18, 2017, Xi Jinping delivered a keynote speech entitled Working Together to Build a Community with a Shared Future for Humanity at the UN Headquarters in Geneva. He once again called on the international community to stay committed to building a world of lasting peace through dialogue and consultation, to build a world of common security for all through joint efforts, to build a world of common prosperity through win-win cooperation, to build an open and inclusive world through exchanges and mutual learning, and to make the world clean and beautiful by pursuing green and low-carbon development. In his report delivered at the 19th National Congress of the CPC in October 2017, President Xi Jinping called on "the people of all countries to work together to build an open, inclusive, clean and beautiful world that enjoys lasting peace, universal security, and common prosperity".*

While actively advocating, enriching and promoting the concept of 'a community with a shared future for humanity', the Chinese government also proposed new concepts such as correctly viewing justice and profit, partnership rather than alliance, a new type of major country relations, global economic governance and new security concepts. These practical and feasible concepts have continuously enriched diplomatic practice with Chinese characteristics, and have been integrated into the system of diplomatic theory with Chinese characteristics.

II. Main Strategies of China's Diplomacy

China's diplomatic strategic thinking mainly consists of global, regional, national, and territorial strategies. It represents the overall framework and planning of its interaction with the rest of the world.

1) Objectives, Missions and Approaches

In terms of China's diplomatic strategies, different historic phases have required different objectives and missions. The Report of the 18th National Congress of the CPC stated that 'judging both current international and domestic environments, China remains in an important era of strategic opportunities for its development, in which much can be achieved. We need to have a correct understanding of the changing nature and conditions of this period, seize all opportunities, respond with consideration to challenges, and obtain the initiative and advantages for the future so as to achieve the goal of completing the building of a moderately prosperous society in all respects by 2020'. Centered on this major target, the overall objectives and missions of China's diplomacy in this period are aimed at creating favorable internal and external environments.

Upholding the banner of peace, development, cooperation and mutual benefit, and adhering to a peaceful path of development are the fundamental approaches of China's diplomatic strategy. They are determined by various factors, such as historical traditions, values orientation, practical interests and realistic needs. Over 40 years of reform and opening up, China has achieved great social and economic progress through peaceful development and has also made active contributions to global peace and stability. Since 2010, both China and the international community have faced unprecedented challenges. In spite of the unpredictable international situation, China will be unswervingly committed to the peaceful path of development and firmly upholding its independent policy of peaceful diplomacy. As a responsible major country in the world, China is certainly well prepared to tackle all sorts of challenges and crises and preserve its national core interests, world peace and stability.

2) Global Strategic Thinking and Arrangements

Each of China's governments in different historical periods have had their own characteristics of global strategic thinking. The global strategic thinking of the Chinese leaders of the first generation, with Mao Zedong at the forefront, focused on preserving national sovereignty and establishing diplomatic relations with other countries. They successively adopted the concept of relying on socialist countries, third-world countries and establishing a triangular strategic relationship between China, the United States, and the Soviet Union to adapt to the international environment of that period. The global strategic thinking of the Chinese leaders of the second generation, led by Deng Xiaoping, focused on opening up and accelerating China's modernization. They mapped out the basic path of reform and opening up. During the upheaval in Eastern Europe and the disintegration of the Soviet Union, Deng Xiaoping promptly proposed the strategic principle of 'keeping a low profile'. The global strategic thinking of the Chinese leaders of the third generation, led by Jiang Zemin, focused on seizing and taking advantage of historical windows of opportunity. They established four strategic arrangements: 'major powers are the key, neighboring countries are the first priority, developing countries are the foundation, and multilateral forums are the important stages' in order to promote China's multidimensional diplomacy.

Between 2002 and 2012, Chinese leaders, with Hu Jintao as General Secretary, made the transition from the 'four strategic arrangements' to the 'five balances', specifically, the balance between nations or regions and territories, between state players and non-state players, between traditional security and non-traditional security, between concrete cooperation and institution building, and between rights preservation and stability preservation. These 'five balances' indicate the rapid development of China's diplomatic relations and overseas interests, and demonstrate the coordination of its diplomatic relations in a more comprehensive and systematic way.

The 18th CPC National Congress held in November 2012 marked the smooth transition from the CPC Central Committee with Comrade Hu Jintao as General Secretary to the CPC Central Committee with Comrade Xi Jinping as the core. The *Report of the 18th Party Congress* reiterated

China's principles and stance on diplomatic relations. China adheres to the independent policy of peaceful diplomacy, which consists of the path of peaceful development and the strategies of opening up, mutual benefit and win-win results. The report, in accordance with the changed situation and mission, has deepened and expanded global strategic thinking by introducing the concepts of 'advocating the awareness of building a human community with a common destiny, pursuing our own interests while taking into account the legitimate concerns of other countries, and promoting the common development of all countries in the course of our own development'.

3) Regional Strategic Thinking and Development

China has two regional strategies – one of which is in a broad sense and the other in a narrow sense. Broadly speaking, China's regional strategies refer to the strategic plans and strategic thinking toward some major regions which are elaborated on in related policies and documents that highlight China's cooperative or strategic partnership with major regions in the world. For example, on October 13, 2003 the Chinese government released *China's Policies and Documents on the European Union*, putting forward the idea of 'China's commitment to building a long-term, stable and comprehensive relationship with Europe'. On January 12, 2006 the Chinese government issued *China's Policies and Documents on Africa*, which states that 'China would continue to enhance the traditional friendship between China and Africa. In the fundamental interests of the Chinese and African people, China will establish and develop a new strategic partnership with African countries featuring equality and mutual trust in politics, cooperation and mutually beneficial results in economics, and exchanges and mutual learning in culture'. On November 5, 2008 China released *China's Policies and Documents on Latin American and Caribbean Countries*, emphasizing the idea that 'the Chinese government would take a strategic perspective on China-Latin America relations, and endeavor to build and develop a comprehensive cooperative partnership based on equality, mutual benefit and common development with Latin American and Caribbean countries'. On November 24, 2016, the Chinese government launched a second and renewed version of *China's Policies and Documents on Latin American and Caribbean Countries*, putting forward that 'China is committed to building a new relationship with Latin America and the Caribbean with five salient features, namely: sincerity and mutual trust in the political field; win-win cooperation on the economic front; mutual learning in culture; close coordination in international affairs; and mutual reinforcement between China's cooperation with the region as a whole and its bilateral relations with individual countries in the region. It aims to bring the comprehensive and cooperative partnership to a new height by bringing the two sides into a community with a shared future in which all countries join hands in development', which provides the progressive policy basis for developing its relations with Latin America and the Caribbean.

In a narrow sense, however, China's regional strategies refer to its strategic plans and thinking regarding neighboring areas. Since reform and opening up, China's regional strategies have evolved into the following main aspects. First, China upholds peace and stability in its peripheral areas. China adheres to the diplomatic policies of 'bringing harmony, security and prosperity to its neighbors'. This highlights the concepts of closeness, sincerity, shared prosperity and inclusiveness in promoting diplomatic relations with them. This will create a favorable peripheral environment for our own development, as well as mutual benefit and win-win results with other countries. China is, and will always be, a good friend, neighbor and partner of ASEAN and Asian countries. China therefore proposes and participates in all sorts of regional security mechanisms, such as the Shanghai Cooperation Organization (SCO), the Six-Party Talks on the North Korean Nuclear Issue, the ASEAN Regional Forum, the Shangri-La Dialogue, and takes an active part in the settlement of regional conflicts. Currently, China's priority is to find a balance between safeguarding national sovereignty in maritime security and preserving regional stability. Second, China is pushing to strengthen practical economic cooperation with its neighboring countries. On the basis of mutual benefit and win-win results, China has made continuous progress on regional economic cooperation and plays a crucial role in 'ASEAN+N' economic cooperation. China has become the major trading partner of most of its neighboring countries. The cooperation between China and some countries on free trade zones and finance is boosting regional economic cooperation. Furthermore, China is ready to consider joining the 'Trans-Pacific Partnership (TPP)' agreement. Third, China is developing its people-to-people exchanges with neighboring countries. In jointly hosting the 'Year of Culture', the 'Year of Language' and the 'Year of Tourism', China contributes to people-to-people exchanges with neighboring countries. People-to-people exchanges together with security and economic cooperation have become the 'three major pillars' within the SCO.

4) An Equal Approach to Country and Field Strategies

China's country strategies mainly comprise the 'big powers strategy', the 'middle powers (namely regional powers) strategy' and the 'strategy for the broad mass of developing countries'. Within China's foreign strategy arrangements, diplomacy with the big powers is listed as the 'key', which includes not only the traditional powers but also the emerging big powers. Bilateral relations between China and the relevant big powers remain China's main concern. Moreover, the interactions with them at regional and global level have become new diplomatic achievements. For example, the interaction between China and European powers such as Germany and France closely resembles cooperation between China and the EU. China and the emerging powers, represented by the BRICS countries, are strengthening their cooperation and interaction through building mechanisms such as the Group of 20 (G20) and climate change. China-US relations are the focus in China's relations with other major countries. The report delivered at the 18th CPC National Congress stated that 'we will strive to establish a new type of relations of long-term stability and sound growth with other major countries', among which the US is a key one. Both China and the US have experienced their leadership succession, and China has repeatedly clarified its resolute rejection of the zero-sum concept and the Cold War mentality, refuting the 'historical fatalism' that the emerging major countries and the traditional ones inevitably are to be in conflicts, or even wars. The China-Russia comprehensive strategic partnership of coordination plays a special role in advancing major country diplomacy with Chinese characteristics. The heads of both sides have maintained close contacts, forging profound friendship and boosting mutual political trust. China and Russia have deepened their practical cooperation in various fields, and have made progress in the areas of economy, commerce, finance and intercultural communication. The two sides have reached new heights in their bilateral ties.

In recent years, the middle powers have received more and more attention in China's foreign strategy. The middle powers include South Korea and Indonesia in East Asia, Saudi Arabia and Turkey in the Middle East, Australia in Oceania, Argentina in South America, and Mexico in North America. There are four reasons why China attaches great importance to them. First, they have very close relations with China as most of them are China's strategic or cooperative partners. Second, they are among the second tier of emerging-market countries, boasting strong economic vitality and highly promising economic prospects. Third, the development of relations between China and the middle powers also sets an example of leadership, which can help strengthen cooperation between China and the regions they belong to. Fourth, their influence in global diplomacy, politics, security and other aspects is increasing constantly, thereby forming a close interaction with China, major powers and developing countries.

The broad group of developing countries are the 'foundation' of China's foreign strategic arrangements. First, they share the same political basis, as China is a developing country with the same or similar history and development direction as other developing countries, so in terms of international system restructuring and reform of the world order they need to resonate and cooperate with each other. Second, they have a shared economic basis. Developing countries have plenty of room for further development and boast a wealth of resources and a rapidly growing market capacity. The above-mentioned areas are the main target destinations for the implementation of China's 'globalization' strategy. Hence they are important partners for China's sustainable development plan. Third, they form the international basis for China to uphold unity. Developing countries are always supportive of China's efforts to safeguard national unity and territorial integrity. They are also supportive of China's diplomatic efforts related to Taiwan, Tibet, Xinjiang and other issues. Last, they represent the moral foundation for maintaining China's diplomacy. China has always held that all countries, big or small, are equal. While maintaining the support of developing countries, China also balances the scales and upholds justice in the international arena. With its continued growth in terms of its comprehensive national strength, China has found it more important to provide developing countries with political, economic, and security support. China has also found it necessary to uphold morality and justice in international relations.

China's field strategy is a new source of growth for its diplomacy. In recent years, the international community has become increasingly concerned about problems in the field such as climate change, financial security, nuclear safety, energy security, resource security, food security and disaster prevention. Therefore, field diplomacy plays an increasingly important role in China's overall diplomacy. With the further enhancement of the nation's overall strength, China is becoming more deeply involved in diplomatic activities in different fields all over the world. In an era of political multi-polarization, economic globalization, cultural diversity and social informatization, China's field strategy provides salutary ideas for the world to respond effectively to global problems together. Moreover, after integrating strategic thinking to include dimensions such as non-traditional diplomacy, new international issues, and global development trends, China is forming more global and progressive ideas. China pays more attention to its field strategy from the perspective of national comprehensive diplomatic strategic arrangements.

Since the beginning of the 21st century, the new task of China's diplomacy has been centered on how to defuse the impact of China's rise on the outside world. China has strategically transformed its system of economic diplomacy into a relatively complete system. It consists of a close integration of diplomacy, the economy, and synchronized progress at the national and regional levels as well as the complementarity of 'inward-facing' and 'outward-facing' strategies. It therefore advances the awareness of mutual economic reliance within the community and sharing trials and tribulations with other countries. China's military diplomacy plays an increasingly significant role in strengthening national political influence, enhancing confidence-building in military security and upgrading the level of multilateral cooperation, which has improved China's image of maintaining international peace. Public diplomacy and cultural diplomacy serve as major platforms for spreading China's ideas, refining core values, leading international public opinion and together improving overall understanding with other countries.

(By Yang Jiemian)

Chapter 2

China's Relations with Neighboring Countries

China's diplomacy with neighboring countries is a priority in its diplomatic agenda. Since the founding of the PRC, Chinese governments have attached great importance to diplomacy with their neighbors. Guided by the policy of good neighborliness and friendliness they have developed a series of important strategic ideas and policies to initiate a generally favorable environment for China's modernization. Since its reform and opening up, the rapid growth of China's economy and the rise of its international status, China's diplomacy with neighboring countries has featured more prominently in China's overall diplomacy. After entering the new century, the Chinese government formally proposed that 'the development of its relationship with neighboring countries should top China's diplomatic agenda'. Whether it is in terms of geographical location, natural environment or mutual relations, the diplomacy with neighboring countries is of extremely important strategic significance to China. Since the 18th CPC National Congress, while maintaining the consistency and stability of diplomatic policies and principles, China has made comprehensive arrangements for its overall diplomacy, highlighting the important role of neighboring countries in China's overall development and diplomacy. In November 2014, the Foreign Affairs Work Conference held by the CPC Central Committee laid more emphasis on diplomacy with neighboring countries and made it the top priority of China's diplomatic strategic arrangements. At the 19th CPC National Congress, it was underlined that China will deepen relations with its neighbors in accordance with the principles of amity, sincerity, mutual benefit, and inclusiveness, and the policy of forging friendship and partnership with its neighbors. China remains firm in its commitment to forging a new form of international relations featuring mutual respect, fairness, justice, and win-win cooperation, and to working to build a community with a shared future for humanity.

I. The Formation and Evolution of China's Good-Neighborly Diplomatic Ideology

China's good-neighborly diplomacy stems from the tradition of loving peace and opposing aggression. Since ancient times China has upheld integrity and good neighborliness and has been willing to treat neighboring countries sincerely and coexist with them on friendly terms. Having good relations with neighbors and friendliness in general are deeply rooted in Chinese cultural tradition.

Mao Zedong and other first-generation CPC leaders laid the ideological foundation for new China's good-neighborly foreign policy. Good-neighborly diplomatic ideology is mainly reflected in two aspects: first, regardless of their size or power, all countries are equal. This is a diplomatic principle established by Mao Zedong which serves as the ideological source for modern China in promoting good-neighborly foreign policy. Second, seeking common ground while setting aside differences is also important. At the Bandung Conference in 1955, on behalf of the PRC, Premier Zhou Enlai, together with the leaders of other Asian and African countries, jointly advocated the Bandung Spirit, which is the pursuit of peaceful co-existence and seeking common ground while setting aside differences. This is an example of China's good-neighborly diplomatic ideology and policy in practice, which has contributed to the harmonious co-existence between modern China and its peripheral countries.

Since reform and opening up, and in particular after the Cold War, China's new generation of leaders have insisted on good-neighborly relations and friendliness in order to develop a favorable environment with its neighbors for China's modernization drive and to serve as a guideline for resolving disputes with neighboring countries. Under the guidance of its good-neighborly diplomatic ideology, China advocates the resolution of controversial problems through friendly consultation and negotiation with its neighbors. As for problems that cannot be solved for the time being, China continues to maintain the policy of 'setting aside the problem temporarily and seeking common ground while shelving differences'. Since the beginning of the 21st century, China has been upholding the policy of forging friendship and partnership with its neighbors, and of fostering an amicable, stable and prosperous neighborhood, which enriches the connotations and measures of the diplomatic thinking of promoting friendship and partnership with its neighbors.

The *Report of the 18th National CPC Congress* highlighted that China would remain committed to good-neighborly diplomacy and stressed that China would work hard to develop itself so as to bring even more benefits to its neighbors. This policy has set the course for China's good-neighborly diplomacy and field diplomacy. At *The Conference on Diplomatic Work with Neighboring Countries* held on October 24, 2013, President Xi Jinping emphasized that the basic principle of China's diplomacy with its neighboring countries was that China would always pursue friendship and partnership with its neighbors and seek to bring friendship, security and common prosperity to its 'neighborhood', thus stressing the concepts of 'intimacy, sincerity, mutual benefit and inclusiveness'.

'Intimacy' here means that China is committed to good-neighborly relations, friendliness and mutual assistance, and that China attaches importance to equality and sincerity, frequently engaging with its neighbors. In addition, China will act more kindly and positively towards neighboring countries to strengthen friendships and gain more recognition and support from them to enhance China's accessibility, appeal and influence. 'Sincerity' refers to the sincere treatment of neighboring countries to attract more friends and partners. 'Mutual benefit' means to base China's cooperation with neighboring countries on mutual benefit, to develop closer networks of common interests and drive the convergence of mutual interests, so that neighboring countries can benefit from China's development, and China in turn can also benefit from the common development of neighboring countries. 'Inclusiveness' refers to the notion of being accommodative. China emphasizes that the Asia-Pacific is large enough to accommodate the common development of all nations in the region, and that China will promote regional cooperation with a more open and positive attitude. These new diplomatic concepts proposed by Xi Jinping have become the guidelines for China's diplomatic policy-making and practice.[1]

China's good-neighborly diplomacy offers a basic policy guide for resolving border disputes. China has the most neighbors along its land borders, the longest boundaries, and the most complex boundary conditions in the world. Its land borders stretch more than 22,000km, shared with 14 countries. In the early days after the founding of the PRC there were land border disputes due to a lack of defined borders with its neighbors. In order to reach a satisfactory solution to border disputes the Chinese government

---

[1] *Xi Jinping: A Speech at the Forum on China's Diplomatic Work with Its Neighbors* [N]. People's Daily, October 26, 2013.

has, for the purpose of its overall and long-term national interests, taken a practical and realistic approach to proposing and following a series of effective principles and methods. This includes firmly safeguarding national sovereignty and territorial integrity, carrying out friendly consultations on an equal basis, seeking fair and reasonable settlement through mutual understanding and accommodation, maintaining the status quo before the problem is solved, taking the historical background and the existing reality into account, dealing with historical border treaties according to the general principles of international law, and following common international practice in defining and settling borders.

On January 24, 1960, Premier Zhou Enlai gave a warm welcome to Mr Ne Win, the Prime Minister of Myanmar (formerly Burma) and his entourage during his goodwill visit to China (photograph by Zheng Xiaozhen, Xinhua News Agency)

In order to advance the settlement of border disputes between China and its neighbors, develop friendly cooperation with them, and create a peaceful and stable peripheral environment for China's economic construction, the Chinese government is committed to the principle of good neighborliness and friendship. This allows the government to address bilateral relations including border issues with its neighboring countries, realize the mutual promotion of good-neighborly relations and friendship, and settle border issues. China has respectively signed border agreements with North Korea, Russia, Kazakhstan, Kyrgyzstan, Tajikistan, Mongolia, Afghanistan, Pakistan, Nepal, Myanmar, Laos and Vietnam, and thoroughly resolved its land border issues with these 12 neighboring countries. These represent the positive results from the implementation of China's good-neighborly diplomatic ideology and policy. India and Bhutan remain the only two countries with which China has not agreed defined land borders. China's continental coastline extends more than 18,000km, adjacent or opposite to the waters of North Korea, South Korea, Japan, the Philippines, Brunei, Indonesia, Malaysia and Vietnam. At present, China has not agreed defined maritime borders with these eight maritime neighbors. Disputes over maritime rights and interests therefore occur from time to time. China hopes to resolve these disputes through peaceful consultation based on mutual understanding and accommodation.

II. China's Economic Relations with Neighboring Countries

China attaches great importance to enhancing regional economic cooperation and strengthening economic ties with its neighboring countries. China proposes to cooperate with neighboring countries according to the principle of mutual benefit, developing closer networks of common interests and strengthening the convergence of mutual interests. This is so that neighboring countries can benefit from China's development, and in turn China can also benefit from the common development of neighboring countries. China has actively promoted economic cooperation with ASEAN countries (10+1), intensified East Asian regional cooperation with the 10+3 countries (ASEAN plus China, Japan and South Korea) as the main channel, and actively participated in the East Asia Summit (EAS). China has also brought forward a series of important initiatives and concepts such as the 'Belt and Road' initiative (the Silk Road Economic Belt and 21st Century Maritime Silk Road) to clarify the direction and implementation path for future development and cooperation between China and its neighboring countries.

1) Economic Cooperation between China and ASEAN Countries (ASEAN+1 or 10+1)

With the acceleration of economic globalization China-ASEAN

economic relations have become increasingly close. This is demonstrated in the most important initiative which is the establishment of a China-ASEAN (ASEAN+1 or 10+1) Free Trade Area (FTA). As early as in 2000, China proposed the establishment of an ASEAN+1 FTA, which received a positive response from ASEAN countries. In 2002 the FTA negotiation was officially launched. In 2004, the Early Harvest Plan of the ASEAN+1 FTA formally came into being. By 2006 the tariff rate for 600 agricultural products was reduced to zero, which indicated that the cooperation between the ASEAN+1 members had achieved initial success. By 2010 China and ASEAN had signed and implemented three key agreements: the *Agreement on Trade in Goods*, the *Agreement on Trade in Services* and the *Agreement on Investment.* In January 2010 the establishment of the ASEAN+1 FTA was completed as scheduled and zero-tariff rates were applied to more than 90% of the products exchanged between China and ASEAN countries. China's average tariff rate on goods from ASEAN countries was dropped from 9.8% to 0.1%, while the average tariff rate of the six original ASEAN member countries on goods from China was reduced from 12.8% to 0.6%. The significant tariff reductions have been a strong stimulus for the fast growth of bilateral trade.

Following the formal establishment of the ASEAN+1 FTA, economic and trade relations between China and ASEAN entered a new stage of development. The total bilateral trade volume exceeded US$400 billion in 2013, US$470 billion in 2015, and is expected to reach US$1 trillion by 2020. The China-ASEAN FTA is the first and also the largest free trade area that China has established with other countries. It is also the first free trade area established by ASEAN as a whole with a foreign country. In October 2013, China proposed to start negotiations on an upgraded version of the China-ASEAN FTA, which was positively responded to by ASEAN. In November 2015, the two sides signed the upgraded protocol, marking the official end of the negotiations. China is making strenuous efforts to carry out the upgraded protocol, in the hope of further enhancing liberalization and facilitation of bilateral trade and investment, and achieving common development.

2) Economic Cooperation between China and ASEAN+3 (10+3)

The cooperation mechanism between the ten ASEAN countries and

China, Japan and South Korea, abbreviated as APT (ASEAN Plus Three), was originated from the idea of an 'East Asia Economic Group' proposed by former Malaysian Prime Minister Mahathir bin Mohamad in the early 1990s. In December 1997, the first APT informal leaders' meeting was held in Kuala Lumpur, which marked the successful launch of the APT cooperation process. The cooperation abides by the principles of being led by ASEAN, seeking consensus through consultations, advancing gradually in due order, accommodating the comfort level of different sides, adhering to mutual respect, equality and mutual benefit, common development, and being open and inclusive. China maintains that ASEAN+3 is the main channel of East Asian cooperation, and this is recognized and supported by other member countries. China believes that APT member countries should play a leading role in the process of building a regional free trade zone and make joint efforts to complete Regional Comprehensive Economic Partnership (RCEP) negotiations as soon as possible. China proposes on its own initiative to eliminate or reduce the debt of poor APT member countries, hoping to set poverty elimination as a priority in the cooperation. China carries out poverty alleviation programs in rural areas, and sets up demonstration programs for poverty reduction cooperation in East Asia. China also advocates the enhancement of exchanges in agricultural technology and cooperation in food security, and the establishment and improvement of the APT Emergency Rice Reserve mechanism, so as to ensure sufficient food supply for all in East Asia. As for prevention and elimination of infectious diseases, China recommended at the 17th APT Summit that national health institutions of the member countries need to enhance communication and cooperation regarding treatment and control of the Ebola epidemic and make joint efforts to improve APT public health systems.[2] China actively promotes the creation of a regional currency cooperation mechanism in the financial field, i.e. the Chiang Mai Initiative on Multilateralization (CMIM), among the member countries. The mechanism has become a self-managed currency swap mechanism in East Asia. With a foreign exchange reserve pool worth US$240 billion, it has laid a foundation for developing higher-level regional financial cooperation.

---

2 Li Keqiang: *Strengthen the Cooperation between China and ASEAN+3 (10+3), Moving Towards a Community with a Shared Future for East Asia[N]*. People's Daily, Nov 14, 2014.

3) The East Asia Summit (EAS)

The East Asia Summit (EAS) is a forum established on the basis of the APT. The establishment of the EAS is seen as a step towards building an East Asian Community. China took an active part in its preparation. ASEAN has set three conditions for countries attending the EAS. First, all participants need to sign the Treaty of Amity and Cooperation in Southeast Asia. Second, participants shall be dialogue partners of ASEAN. Third, participants shall have substantial cooperation with ASEAN. After accepting these conditions, India, Australia and New Zealand attended the first EAS, held on December 14, 2005 in Kuala Lumpur, Malaysia. Russia and the United States formally joined the EAS in October 2010, and their presidents attended the summit the following year. The EAS now has a total of 18 members, and had held 11 summits by the end of 2016. Chinese premiers attended all the previous EASs and exchanged in-depth views with participants in advancing mutual benefit and friendliness, and deepening regional cooperation. China vigorously promotes strategic dialogue among member countries, and encourages cooperation in six key areas including energy and environmental protection, finance, education, public health, disaster management and ASEAN connectivity. Thus, China has played a positive role in increasing mutual trust among participants and facilitating regional cooperation. China supports strengthened cooperation on non-traditional security issues, e.g. anti-terrorism, infectious disease control and prevention, climate change, and disaster management, within the framework of the EAS.

4) The 'Belt and Road' Initiative

The 'Belt and Road' is short for the 'Silk Road Economic Belt' and the '21st Century Maritime Silk Road'. This is a strategic cooperation initiative proposed by President Xi Jinping during his visits to Central Asia and Southeast Asia in September and October 2013. The Silk Road first emerged in China. Meandering through the vast Asian continent and mighty oceans, it links China with other countries in Asia, Africa and Europe. The Belt and Road Initiative carries forward the Silk Road spirit embodied in solidarity and mutual trust, equality and mutual benefit, inclusiveness, a disposition to learn from each other, and cooperation in finding win-win solutions. The Belt and Road Initiative promotes policy coordination, connectivity of infrastructure, unimpeded trade, currency convertibility, and closer people-to-people ties, namely, a 'Five-pronged approach'. Policy coordination mainly involves inter-governmental communication on macroeconomic policy.

Connectivity of infrastructure means the communication of transport and infrastructure. For example, China provided aid to build the railway from Kunming, China to Bangkok, Thailand, and December 2013 saw the closure of the bridge over the Mekong River. China Ocean Shipping Company constructed the well-run container terminals at the port of Piraeus, Greece. China will jointly build railways with Hungary, Serbia, and Turkey. China and Russia have proposed a construction project along the Beijing-Moscow Eurasian express transport corridor. All these will be main concerns of the connectivity of infrastructure. Smooth trading with these countries reflects the immediate relevance of the Silk Road as a channel for commerce. In 2013 the trade volume between China and countries along the route exceeded US$1 trillion. This accounted for a quarter of China's total foreign trade. Trade between China and countries along the route will enjoy a huge volume of growth in the future. China and ASEAN countries plan to increase their bilateral trade volume to US$1 trillion by 2020. Financial integration is to enhance cooperation in the financial field. The Chiang Mai Initiative is a concrete example of this. Understanding among peoples reinforces personnel exchanges and promotes cooperation in the areas of culture, art, archeology, sports and healthcare, including exchanges at sub-national level and between media organizations, think tanks and youth organizations.

III. China's Political Relations with Neighboring Countries

China has generally shared the same historical experiences as most of its neighbors who have suffered the aggression of Western colonialism, demanded respect for their national sovereignty and dignity since the end of the Second World War, and sought common development and promoted cooperation since the end of the Cold War. This has formed a solid foundation for the development of political relations between China and its neighbors. Since the end of the Cold War, the political relationship between China and its neighboring countries has enjoyed stable development through friendly exchanges, and the two sides have become increasingly interdependent. At present, China and its neighboring countries engage in a broad and comprehensive range of high-level exchanges through their contacts at the national leadership and government level. Of course, not all traditional territorial issues have been completely resolved, and meanwhile new concerns have emerged in political relations between China and its neighbors. China therefore needs to appropriately deal with sensitive issues such as land borders and maritime territorial disputes with the countries concerned.

1) Strategic Thinking Behind Developing Political Relations

China's political strategic thinking on promoting neighborhood diplomacy is as follows:

(1) Its aims are driven by and must contribute to the realization of the 'Two Centenary Goals' and the renaissance of the Chinese nation.

To this end, China's neighborhood diplomacy must ensure a favorable period of significant strategic opportunities for national development, safeguard national sovereignty, security and development interests, and strive to engage in more friendly political relations, more solid economic ties, in-depth security cooperation, and closer cultural exchanges with neighboring countries.

(2) China must establish an inclusive ideology which emphasizes the fact that the Asia-Pacific has sufficient space to accommodate the common development of all countries in this region, and it must be more open and active in promoting regional cooperation.

To this end, China stresses that it must implement what it has advocated, so as to realize a common philosophy and code of conduct that can be followed and upheld by countries in the region.

(3) China's establishment of political relations with other countries is not determined by their ideologies and social systems.

China opposes the notion of rejecting other civilizations and cultures. China also opposes any intention or practice of imposing 'values alliances' (alliances based on shared values), and instead encourages dialogue and exchange among different peoples in peripheral areas to prevent doubt and estrangement.

(4) China looks to build new political relationships with all its neighbors according to the principle of nonalignment.

On the basis of seeking common interests and on the premise of nonconfrontation, China is building a framework of new diplomatic relations characterized by nonalignment, cooperation, not being controlled by any third party, mutual benefit and joint efforts to create a better future. China and Russia have developed a comprehensive and strategic partnership of coordination featuring equality, trust, mutual support, common prosperity and lasting friendship.

China has fostered a partnership with ASEAN countries based on mutual trust, created a constructive and reciprocal partnership with India, and made good-neighborly and friendly partnerships of mutual advantage and mutually beneficial cooperation with Pakistan, South Korea and Thailand. China has established a strategic cooperative partnership of coordination for the 21st century with Russia, the 21st century good-neighborly partnership of mutual trust and strategic partnership oriented toward peace and prosperity with ASEAN countries, a strategic partnership oriented toward peace and prosperity with India, an all-weather strategic partnership with Pakistan, and a partnership highlighting good-neighborly friendship and mutually beneficial cooperation with South Korea and Thailand.

(5) China's basic policy of diplomacy with its neighbors is to uphold the combined principles of friendship, sincerity, reciprocity and inclusiveness.

By adhering to these principles, China will help its neighbors in times of difficulty, treat them as equals, and visit them frequently. It will take action to gain and develop closer friendships, more recognition and support, and thereby enhance China's accessibility, appeal and influence.

(6) China proposes to cooperate with its neighboring countries under the principles of reciprocity, more closely-knit networks of common interests, and deepening the convergence of mutual interests, so that neighboring countries can benefit from China's development and China can in turn obtain benefits and impetus from the common development of neighboring countries.

2) New Measures for Creating a Harmonious Environment with China's Neighbors and Promoting Regional Stability

Before and after the end of the Cold War, dramatic changes in the Soviet Union and Eastern Europe led to a significant change in the balance of power between the East and West. Subsequently, the pattern of international relations experienced profound changes. In order to create a favorable international and peripheral environment, China has since put forward new ideas and initiatives for the promotion of regional stability.

First, China developed the diplomatic strategy of 'keeping a low profile'. China brought forward this diplomatic strategy to deal with the complexity of the political situation of the late 1980s and early 1990s, which was characterized by the end of the Cold War and the violent changes in the Soviet Union and Eastern Europe. This diplomatic strategy consists of a series of thoughts to address different kinds of relationships, which can be briefly summarized as the 'Four don'ts' and 'Two transcendences'. The 'Four don'ts' are: 'Don't be an advocate', which means that China adheres to the path of socialism with Chinese characteristics, but is not an advocate of the international communist movement; 'Don't take the lead', which means that although China speaks for developing countries on the international stage, it does not seek to be their leader; 'Don't make enemies', which means that while holding its own views on the changes in the Soviet Union and Eastern Europe, China will maintain normal state-to-state relations with the newly independent Eastern European countries on the basis of the 'Five Principles of Peaceful Coexistence', and will not make enemies of them; and 'Don't confront other nations', which means that when the United States and Western countries undermine its sovereignty, China will resolutely fight for its national interests, yet will refrain from waging a war against them or confronting them. The 'Two transcendences' refers to 'Transcending ideology', which means that the standard of formulating foreign policy will not be determined by ideology but by whether the relevant state has been recognized by its own people, and 'Transcending conventions', which means that when it comes to some issues where China's direct interests are not directly involved, China should assume an attitude of moderate detachment to a certain extent while still adhering to its basic principles, so as to avoid becoming the focus of conflicts. This diplomatic strategy has enabled China to quickly break away from the grip of Western sanctions and rid itself of the extremely difficult international situation China faced in the early period immediately after the end of the Cold War, thus creating a favorable external environment for China's domestic economic development.

Second, China has deepened its political relations with ASEAN countries. China has 11 neighboring countries along its southeastern border[3]. Some small and medium-sized countries were apprehensive towards China due to historical grievances and disputes over territory and maritime rights and interests. After the Cold War, China made great efforts to improve relations with neighboring countries. In 1991, China established diplomatic relations

---

3. *The 11 countries in Southeast Asia refer to the 10 ASEAN countries and East Timor. East Timor won independence from Indonesia in 1999 and formally established the Democratic Republic of East Timor in 2002. In the same year, East Timor established diplomatic relations with China. East Timor is currently applying for membership of ASEAN.*

with 10 ASEAN countries, and respectively signed political documents with each of them focused on developing bilateral relations for the 21st century. Since the establishment of the China-ASEAN strategic partnership in 2003, mutual political trust between the two sides has deepened, with both sides supporting each other on many major international and regional issues and maintaining good neighborliness, friendliness and harmonious coexistence. The decade (2003-2013) is known as the 'golden decade' of China-ASEAN relations.

Since 2013, China-ASEAN relations have entered a new stage. China has put forward the idea of building a China-ASEAN community of interest and the 21st Century Maritime Silk Road, and a '2 + 7 cooperation framework' which refers to the two political consensuses on deepening strategic mutual trust and expanding friendship, and focusing on economic development to promote mutual benefit and win-win cooperation, and the seven priority areas that include the political, economic and trade, connectivity, finance, maritime, security and cultural fields. China has also explored negotiating with ASEAN to conclude a bilateral treaty of good-neighborliness, friendship and cooperation. China and ASEAN have celebrated achievements made in the 'Golden Decade' of strategic partnership, and on this basis, ushered in a 'Diamond Decade'.

Third, China has promoted the six-party talks on the North Korea nuclear issue. The Korean peninsula borders China, and is a very close neighboring region to China. In the early 1990s and at the start of this century, North Korean nuclear crises broke out twice. The Chinese government made multilateral mediation to seek a peaceful resolution of the nuclear issue, and managed to establish the mechanism of six-party talks on this issue in August 2003. The talks have been conducted six times so far, and have been at a standstill due to various complicated reasons. China's policies on the North Korea nuclear issue are to maintain peace and stability on the Korean peninsula, to achieve denuclearization of the Korean peninsula, and to persist in solving the problem through dialogue and negotiations. China not only maintains normal relations with North Korea, but also develops a cooperative partnership with South Korea. China stands firmly opposed to North Korea's nuclear tests. China opposes nuclear proliferation and all actions that may further worsen the situation. China hopes other parties concerned return to the track of six-party talks and create a favorable external environment for the peaceful settlement of affairs on the peninsula. China will continue to make unremitting efforts to safeguard peace and stability in Northeast Asia.

Fourth, China actively maintains good-neighborly and friendly relations with the five central Asian countries of Kazakhstan, Kyrgyzstan, Tajikistan, Uzbekistan and Turkmenistan. Among them, Kazakhstan, Kyrgyzstan and Tajikistan share borders with China. The border spans more than 3,000km. Although Uzbekistan and Turkmenistan share no direct borders with China, they are geographically close to China, and have a very long history of exchange and relations with China.

China develops relations with these five Central Asian countries on the basis of the Five Principles of Peaceful Coexistence. China carries out cooperation with them based on equality. China joins hands with Central Asian countries to cope with regional security challenges, so as to safeguard peace and tranquility in Central Asia and make joint efforts to fight against the 'Three forces' including 'East Turkistan'. At the same time, China actively conducts cultural exchanges and continuously enhances people-to-people friendship.

China maintains close coordination and communication with these five Central Asian countries on a bilateral and multilateral basis. China and Kazakhstan hold the same stand on many important international and regional affairs, and enjoy high-level political mutual trust, so the two countries have made strategic docking for their development, and further enhanced cooperation in key areas such as energy, capacity, transportation and agriculture. China and Kyrgyzstan established a strategic partnership in 2013. China respects the balanced and pragmatic foreign policy pursued by Kyrgyzstan. Both countries enjoy sound cooperation in fighting against international terrorism, extremism and separatism. China and Kyrgyzstan concentrate on cooperation in energy, electricity and infrastructure construction. Since China and Tajikistan established diplomatic ties in 1992, bilateral relations have been developing steadily, and the two sides have become good neighbors, good friends and good partners. In 2013, the two countries established a strategic partnership. China and Tajikistan have strengthened law enforcement, security and defense cooperation, and jointly combat the 'Three forces', drug trafficking and transnational crime. Both sides cooperate on the China-Central Asia gas pipeline project, and other projects such as the transformation of Tajikistan's electric transmission and distribution grid, transportation and border infrastructure construction, industrial parks, and agricultural technology demonstration parks. China and Turkmenistan established diplomatic relations in 1992. China respects Turkmenistan's permanently neutral foreign policy. Bilateral relations were raised to a strategic partnership in 2013. The two sides maintain close communication and coordination in fighting against the 'Three forces' and safeguarding regional security and stability. China is the largest natural gas export market of Turkmenistan, and the two sides have achieved fruitful results in the field of natural gas cooperation. China and Uzbekistan established diplomatic ties in 1992. Since then, bilateral relations have developed smoothly. In 2012, the two countries established a strategic partnership. China respects Uzbekistan's equilibrium strategy with other big countries. China has strengthened its cooperation with Uzbekistan in the field of energy, finance, agriculture and transportation infrastructure construction, and is focused on the construction and operation of the China-Central Asia gas pipeline, and actively promotes the China-Kyrgyzstan-Uzbekistan railway project.

Fifth, China is further developing an 'all-weather strategic cooperative partnership' with Pakistan, an important neighbor to the west of China. Since the establishment of diplomatic relations in 1951, China has adhered to the 'Five Principles of Peaceful Coexistence'. The basic polices of China to strengthen relations with Pakistan are as follows: China respects the independence, sovereignty and territorial integrity of Pakistan, appreciates and supports Pakistan in addressing issues with its neighboring countries through peaceful settlement and all of its efforts to safeguard national sovereignty, territorial integrity and independence. China has promised not to cooperate with any league or group, nor to conclude any treaties with third countries that threaten Pakistan's sovereignty, security and territorial integrity. Nor will China allow a third country to use its territory to harm Pakistan's sovereignty, security and territorial integrity. China and Pakistan have pledged to strengthen trust and cooperation in terms of defense and security, which together they aim to consolidate. The good-neighborly and friendly relationship between China and Pakistan is not targeted against any third country. In following the above principles and ideas, China and Pakistan maintain regular high-level strategic dialogue and mutual visits, and China-Pakistan relations have developed into 'bosom friends and all-weather strategic cooperative partners'.[4]

In 2013, during his visit to Pakistan, Premier Li Keqiang announced that China and Pakistan would jointly build a 'China-Pakistan Economic Corridor'. The long-term plan for the 'China-Pakistan Economic Corridor', in addition to opening up roads, railways, oil and gas pipelines and fiber optic cables, will also include alleviating Pakistan's electricity shortage, and

---

4. Xi Jinping met with the Prime Minister of Pakistan: China and Pakistan are 'all-weather strategic cooperative partners' (http://cpc.people.com.cn/n/2014/1108/c64094-25996113.html)(2017-11-12)

support construction projects to facilitate people's livelihood (e.g. the use of water and the disposal of sewage and garbage), thus making the corridor 'a development path' that will truly benefit the local people. At the same time, the 'China-Pakistan Economic Corridor' will closely link South Asia, Central Asia and the Middle East, stimulating strong economic growth and providing a cooperation platform for interconnectivity to the areas on China's western periphery.

3) Active Participation in Multilateral Diplomacy with China's Neighbors

China's multilateral diplomacy mainly refers to participation in multilateral diplomatic activities organized by international organizations or within a framework of regional arrangements. During the first three decades after the founding of the new PRC, with the exception of its attendance at the Bandung Conference, China did not participate in multilateral diplomatic activities in its peripheral areas, and instead focused on bilateral diplomacy. After the Cold War, China emphasized multilateral diplomacy in peripheral areas, and began to gradually integrate into the periphery and participate in multilateral diplomatic activities in peripheral areas. With the establishment of the WTO and the accelerating process of globalization, in order to adapt to the trend of economic globalization and actively participate in international economic cooperation and competition, China has adjusted its foreign policy, taken part in various multilateral cooperation mechanisms and made full use of the favorable conditions and opportunities brought about by economic globalization.

The basic philosophy and policies China adheres to in this process are as follows: China maintains the principles of independence and sovereign equality, opposes any international organization or country that employs an international mechanism to interfere with China's internal affairs, as well as any intervention in the internal affairs of any other country. Regarding the Taiwan issue, China opposes any intergovernmental or international organization that accepts Taiwan's participation. China always adheres to the policy of nonalignment, and remains committed to its principles of openness and not targeting any third party while participating in or establishing international organizations. China maintains its identity and position as a developing country, and speaks for developing countries.

In its diplomatic activities with its neighbors, China has participated in, or proposed the setting up of, many multilateral cooperation mechanisms, including ASEAN, the Asia-Pacific Economic Cooperation (APEC) and Shanghai Cooperation Organization (SCO), Regional Comprehensive Economic Partnership (RCEP) and Conference on Interaction and Confidence-Building Measures in Asia (CICA).

(1) China takes part in multilateral diplomatic activities with ASEAN. Under the shadow of the Cold War, when ASEAN, a regional organization for multilateral cooperation, was newly established, ASEAN and China lacked mutual trust and doubted each other. China-ASEAN relations gradually eased in the early 1970s. In the early 1990s, China realized the normalization of relations with all ASEAN members, and China-ASEAN dialogue officially began. In 1996, China became a full dialogue partner of ASEAN. After the Asian financial crisis in 1997, China and ASEAN established a good-neighborly partnership of mutual trust for the 21st century. China signed the *Declaration on the Conduct of Parties in the South China Sea* with ASEAN in 2002. In 2003, the Chinese government announced its accession to the *Treaty of Friendship and Cooperation in Southeast Asia*, and China became the first ASEAN dialogue partner to ratify the treaty. Also, in the same year, China and ASEAN announced the establishment of a strategic partnership oriented toward peace and prosperity. China maintains frequent high-level exchanges with ASEAN; Chinese leaders have attended all previous China-ASEAN summits, and ASEAN leaders regularly visit China. In 2010, following the successful implementation of the first *Plan of Action to Implement the Joint Declaration on the China-ASEAN Strategic Partnership for Peace and Prosperity (2005-2010)*, the two sides formulated the second Action Plan for the period 2011-2015.[5] The current Chinese government attaches greater importance to participation in multilateral diplomacy with ASEAN, and is willing to prioritize ASEAN in its neighborhood diplomacy, supporting its development and expansion. China firmly supports ASEAN in promoting the community and integration processes, and firmly supports the leading role of ASEAN in regional cooperation. China stands ready to consolidate and deepen its strategic partnership with ASEAN, and to vigorously facilitate all key cooperation projects and promote peace, stability and prosperity in the region.

(2) China advances the establishment of the SCO. The Shanghai Cooperation Organization (SCO), established by the UN with its secretariat operating in China, is an inter-governmental organization,

---

5. *The Ministry of Foreign Affairs of the PRC. China-ASEAN Cooperation: 1991-2011* [M]. Xinhua News Agency, Beijing, November 15, 2011

which grew out of the 'Shanghai Five' mechanism. On June 15, 2001, the heads of six countries, China, Russia, Kazakhstan, Kyrgyzstan, Tajikistan and Uzbekistan respectively, met in Shanghai and signed the *Declaration on the Shanghai Cooperation Organization*, signifying the founding of the SCO. The SCO's mission is to strenghten friendship and trust among member states, encourage effective cooperation, safeguard regional peace and stability, boost the economic development of the region and member states, and promote a new international political and economic order that is fair and just. The SCO advocates the 'Shanghai spirit' of mutual trust, mutual benefit, equality, consultation, respect for cultural diversity and the pursuit of common development. In August 2007, the state leaders signed the *Treaty on Long-term Good-Neighborliness, Friendship and Cooperation of SCO Member Countries*. The key cooperation areas of the SCO are in security, including jointly combating the three forces of terrorism, separatism and extremism, and signing relevant treaties for economic and cultural cooperation. The member states signed the relevant documents concerning cooperation on education, culture, health and other areas. China hopes that the SCO can be built into an important force for peace, development and cooperation in Eurasia, that the SCO will strengthen cooperation in the areas of security, economy and culture, and that the member states will work together to maintain regional security and stability while promoting common prosperity and development.

(3) China and Asia-Pacific Economic Cooperation (APEC). The APEC forum is the highest-level mechanism for economic cooperation in the Asia-Pacific region. It covers the most extensive part of the world and wields significant influence. China joined APEC in 1991. Since 1993 when the mechanism for APEC economic leaders' meetings was set up, Chinese leaders have attended all of them. China also hosted two APEC Summit meetings, once in Shanghai in 2001 and the other in Beijing in 2014, demonstrating its important and constructive role in APEC's development. Economically, China and the Asia-Pacific region promote mutual growth. In 2013, trade between China and other APEC members reached US$2.5 trillion, accounting for 60% of China's total foreign trade. Eight out of China's top 10 trading partners are APEC members. In 2013, China's direct investment in APEC member states accounted for 69% of China's total foreign direct investment (FDI), and FDI from APEC members in turn accounted for 83% of China's total utilized foreign capital.

In 2014, the 22nd APEC economic leaders' meeting was held in Beijing, and President Xi Jinping attended and chaired the meeting. The meeting focused on the theme of 'Shaping the Future Through Asia-Pacific Partnership' and on three major themes: 'Advancing Regional Economic Integration', 'Promoting Innovative Development, Economic Reform and Growth', and 'Enhancing Comprehensive Connectivity and Infrastructure Development'. The member states discussed regional economic cooperation and their vision of Asia-Pacific development. The meeting issued two documents. One was *The Beijing Agenda for an Integrated, Innovative and Interconnected Asia-Pacific—the 22nd APEC Economic Leaders' Declaration*, and the other was *Shaping the Future through Asia-Pacific Partnership—Statement on the 25th Anniversary of APEC*. The meeting encouraged member states to work jointly for an Asia-Pacific economic environment which is open, inclusive, balanced and beneficial to all, and to achieve common development, progress and prosperity. Meanwhile, it envisaged a new vision for long-term Asia-Pacific economic development. In the meeting, the APEC members decided to launch and advance the process of the Free Trade Area of the Asia-Pacific (FTAAP), approved *The Roadmap for APEC's Contribution to the Realization of the FTAAP*, and adopted *The APEC Accord on Innovative Development, Economic Reform and Growth*, which has injected new impetus into the economic growth of the Asia-Pacific and further consolidated the Asia-Pacific's position as the engine of the global economy. The 22nd APEC economic leaders' meeting in Beijing shows that China will make greater efforts to ensure that China's development and the world's development are mutually reinforcing, and that China will continue to play an even greater role in regional and international affairs as a major responsible country.

IV. China's Security Relationship with Peripheral Countries

The 21st century has seen increasing turbulence in China's neighboring areas. China fully respects the reality of regional diversity and interdependence, and guided by the Asian security concept will address differences from a strategic position and with a long-term perspective, so as to maintain peace, stability and prosperity in the Asia-Pacific.

1) China Advocates the Asian Security Concept and a Defensive National Defense Policy

China upholds the banner of peace, development, cooperation and win-win results, and advocates the Asian security concept with common security, overall security, cooperative security and sustainable security as the core. Common security is respecting and safeguarding the security of every country, as security should be universal. Comprehensive security is to safeguard traditional and non-traditional security as a whole. The security governance of peripheral areas should take into account all factors, such as the historical background and the current circumstances of Asian nations, and should act comprehensively to progress in a coordinated manner. Cooperative security is to promote the solidarity between regions and countries through dialogue and cooperation so as to address the security challenges together and to ensure regional security. Sustainable security is to value both economic development and security to achieve long-term security. It is necessary to promote common development and regional integration in order to maintain synergy between economic cooperation and security cooperation.

China pursues a national defense policy which is defensive in nature. This policy is made according to China's development path and is determined by its fundamental aims and foreign policy, as well as by its historical and cultural traditions. As the situation changes in this new era, China has enriched its national defense policy, increasing its defense forces. For example, China's first aircraft carrier 'Liaoning' was deployed by the Chinese navy on September 25, 2012. Despite the deployment of these new assets, China retains its spirit of rationality and restraint, maintaining defense and peaceful development as its core ideology. China's modernization of its national defense and armed forces has been improving in tandem with its rapid economic and social development, but remains entirely for the purpose of self-defense. China is committed to the path of peaceful development, strives to build a harmonious socialist society domestically, and promotes building a harmonious world of lasting peace and common prosperity externally. China values peace above all else, advocates the settlement of disputes via non-military means, is cautious in its response to military conflicts, and instead maintains the strategy of 'attacking only after being attacked'. China will never seek hegemony, nor will it adopt the approach of military expansion now or in the future, no matter how its economy develops.

2) China's Policy on Peripheral Region Security Issues

(1) Promoting stability and security in peripheral regions through economic cooperation.

The Chinese government advocates the realization of peace and security in Asia through economic cooperation and the promotion of regional economic integration. China firmly believes that regional economic cooperation can further integrate interests, strengthen communication, reinforce mutual trust, and as a result consolidate the foundation for Asia's common development and prosperity.

(2) Promoting security in the Asia-Pacific region through the encouragement of positive interaction among major powers.

The Chinese government believes that the major powers should view each other's strategic intent in a rational and objective way, abandon the Cold War mentality, and cooperatively address regional and global challenges.

(3) Dealing with differences and controversies in an appropriate way.

Many of the controversies centered around China's peripheral areas are a result of a history which victimized China and many other regions and nations. China advocates peaceful and proper treatment of these issues through negotiation and consultation to prevent them from causing more harm. Asian countries have gathered much successful experience in this regard, such as the method of 'quiet diplomacy' adopted by ASEAN, which should be applied in the handling of such differences and disputes. China objects to irrelevant parties being brought into disputes or unilateral resort to international arbitration, as these practices cannot solve the fundamental problem. On the issues of the South and the East China Sea, China is willing to continue to resolve the territorial and maritime rights disputes through negotiation and consultation directly with those parties concerned, on the basis of respecting the historical facts and international law. China will continue to call for 'setting aside disputes for the purpose of joint development', and will fully and effectively implement the *Declaration on the Conduct of Parties in the South China Sea* together with ASEAN countries, while promoting consultation on 'the code of conduct on the South China Sea', so as to maintain peace and stability in the area.

(4) Improving regional multilateral mechanisms and building new security architecture.

China is insistent on multilateralism and is opposed to forming a military alliance against a third party. Using the Asian security concept as guidance, China and other Asian countries will gradually build an Asian security cooperation mechanism that meets the demands of all regions and parties. For this reason, China firmly supports that ASEAN-led mechanisms such as forums and ASEAN Defense Ministers' Expanded Meetings play a larger role in promoting regional security and cooperation. In recent years, China has undertaken almost one-third of the cooperation projects, which involve disaster relief, anti-terrorism, combating transnational crimes, maritime security, preventive diplomacy, and network security under the framework of the ASEAN Regional Forum. Thus, China has made great contributions to deepening cooperation.

(5) The origin of Sino-India border issues and China's related policies.

According to China, there has been no previous demarcation of the Sino-India border, nor have there been any related legal documents which do so, yet there is indeed a traditional and customary border of about 2,000km between China and India. The Indian government, however, believes that most of the Sino-India border was demarcated during Britain's rule of India, which shows a difference of approximately 125,000sq km from that proposed by China. In the late 1950s, India refused to engage in consultations with China on border issues. At his meeting with Prime Minister Nehru during his visit to India in April 1960, the then-premier of China, Zhou Enlai, made six suggestions, including that both sides retain their line of actual control and, as a prerequisite, refrain from mentioning any territorial claim in order to settle the dispute. However, India turned down China's suggestions, leading to the failure of the meeting and the worsening of the border situation. Military conflicts occurred along the Sino-India border in 1962 due to India's unrealistic approach toward the border dispute. In the mid-1990s, China and India reached an agreement on peacekeeping along the line of actual control and confidence-building measures. In 1998, however, India conducted an underground nuclear test as a response to what it identified as 'the China threat', again jeopardizing Sino-Indian relations. In April 2005, China and India jointly signed the *Protocol on Modalities for the Implementation of Confidence-Building Measures in the Military Field Along the Line of Actual Control in the India-China Border Areas*, agreeing on specific implementation measures for certain articles in the 1996 agreement. China is committed to settling border issues at an early stage, which is not only in the interests of both sides, but also beneficial to regional peace and stability. China advocates the settlement of all disputes through peaceful and friendly consultation and the pursuit of a solution that is fair, reasonable and acceptable to both sides. China's new leaders are willing to implement the agreement signed with India in April 2005 on the guiding political principles of settling border issues. Both sides also agree on the important role of the special representative mechanism which was established for the political settlement of the border disputes, as well as the consultation and coordination mechanisms established for the settlement of Sino-Indian border issues.

(6) China's policies and proposals toward the Afghanistan issue.

The Chinese government supports an early realization of Afghanistan's peaceful development and has shown its willingness to accept its responsibilities as one of Afghanistan's neighboring countries. China's fundamental policy is as follows: the peaceful reconstruction process should adhere to the principle that the country 'is owned and controlled by the Afghans'. The independence, sovereignty and territorial integrity of Afghanistan should be respected, as should the rights of the Afghan government and its people. China supports Afghanistan in the strengthening of its sovereignty, autonomy and development, and in promoting national reconciliation independently and creating a favorable environment for the realization of reconciliation. After the removal of the US and NATO forces, the international community should continue to fulfill its commitment to Afghanistan, providing support and assistance with no attached conditions so as to enhance Afghanistan's sustainable development. Existing international organizations and cooperation mechanisms such as the SCO should fully play their roles in supporting Afghanistan's development of foreign relations.

2014 was an important year of transformation in terms of the social reconstruction of Afghanistan. With the successive withdrawal of US and NATO forces, Afghanistan held a presidential election. It is the objective of China's policy that Afghanistan becomes a unified, stable, growing and friendly neighboring country. China advocates that political reconciliation is the important foundation for the peaceful reconstruction of Afghanistan, as well as being fundamental for the realization of Afghanistan's enduring peace and stability. China sincerely calls on all political parties in Afghanistan - including the Taliban - to seize this opportunity, make the right decisions, put aside their differences, focus on the future and reach political reconciliation as soon as possible for the joint discussion on Afghanistan's grand project of peace and development. China firmly supports the peaceful reconciliation of Afghanistan and is willing to continue to play a constructive role.

3) China's Military Confidence-Building Mechanism with Peripheral Countries

China's fundamental policy and principle is to heed the core interests of others and their major concerns on the basis of mutual respect and equality, and to comprehensively and accurately grasp others' strategic intentions on the basis of mutual understanding and confidence-building. The Chinese government believes that military confidence-building is an effective way to maintain national security and development, and also safeguard regional peace and stability. With mutual trust as the groundwork and common security as the goal, China promotes the establishment of equal, mutually beneficial and effective mechanisms for military confidence-building, which should be based on the principles of holding consultations on an equal footing, mutual respect for core interests and recognition of major security concerns, not targeting any third country, nor threatening or harming the security and stability of any other country.

(1) The mechanism of strategic consultation and dialogue.

China has established mechanisms for defense and security consultation and dialogue with 22 countries. China established a strategic consultation mechanism with Russia in 1997. China also maintains consultation with the United States on issues such as non-proliferation, counter-terrorism and bilateral military and security cooperation. China has established mechanisms for defense and security consultation and dialogue with peripheral countries and signed agreements on cooperation and confidence-building in border defense with them.

(2) The mechanism of dialogue and cooperation on maritime security.

China takes an active part in dialogue and cooperation on international maritime security. It strictly complies with the *UN Charter and the UN Convention on the Law of the Sea (UNCLOS)* as well as other universally recognized regulations. China consistently pursues common security and development, and respects the sovereignty, rights and interests of coastal states. China perseveres in dealing with traditional and non-traditional maritime threats through cooperation and strives to maintain maritime security through multiple peaceful ways. In 1998, China and the United States set up a maritime military security consultation mechanism. In October 2005, China and Vietnam signed the *Agreement on Joint Patrols by the Navies of China and Vietnam in the Beibu Gulf.* In February 2009, direct telephone links were officially established between the Chinese and South Korean navy and air forces stationed in adjacent areas. Since 2008,

China and Japan have held several consultations over the establishment of a maritime liaison mechanism. The Chinese Navy has taken an active part in the activities of the Western Pacific Naval Symposium, and held and attended ASEAN Regional Forums, and participated in maritime security cooperation projects.

(By Cai Penghong)

Chapter 3

The Development of China's Diplomacy with Big Countries

Developing diplomatic relations with big countries is key in China's overall diplomacy. Ever since the founding of the PRC, great importance has been attached to diplomacy with big countries, particularly with the major global powers. Prior to the reform and opening-up policy established in 1978, China had successively implemented its strategic measures of 'leaning to one side' (allying with the Soviet Union), using 'two fists' (confronting both the Soviet Union and the United States) and 'rapprochement' (working in coalition with the United States against the Soviet Union), focusing on big country diplomacy throughout, which deeply influenced new China's overall perspective on the external strategic environment. Despite tremendous changes in China's strategic goals and the enrichment of diplomatic connotations and extensions, diplomacy with big countries has remained central to China's overall diplomatic strategy over the past 40 years since reform and opening up. Since the turn of the new millennium, the Chinese government has officially confirmed that 'the major powers are the key'. This is not only because big countries are the most important forces influencing the system of international relations but also because healthy and stable relations with big countries ensure the external environment needed for China's reform and opening up. In November 2012, the *Report of the 18th National Congress of the CPC* introduced the strategic concept of 'establishing long-term stability and sound growth with other big countries', indicating the Chinese government's reflection and practice in a new context of avoiding the clichéd cycle of the rise and fall of major powers as well as the zero-sum game, and to instead cooperatively contribute more material and spiritual wealth to the world's peaceful development.

I. Changes in China's Diplomacy with Big Countries

1) Deepening of Strategic Positioning

China's diplomacy with big Western countries is an integral part of China's big country diplomacy. Ever since the reform and opening up, it has been the prerequisite for China's economic development and opening to the outside world to maintain a generally stable and healthy relationship with big Western countries. Since the start of the 21st century, China has intensified the strategic positioning of its diplomacy with big Western countries, as evidenced in the following respects.

(1) In terms of economic and trade relations, the interdependence between China and big Western countries has been further increased.

On the one hand, developed Western economies continue to be China's most important supplier of technology and management, and its main source of investment, as well as the targeted markets for China's manufactured export goods. On the other hand, with China's industrial development and the significant strengthening of its international competitiveness, China and developed Western countries are experiencing increased economic competition while intensifying industrial cooperation. At the same time, the West is still suffering from the continued impacts of the financial crisis and the European debt crisis. China's increased investment in developed Western countries benefits the West in its recovery from the crisis. It may also raise concerns of China taking the opportunity to seize Western market share and squeeze local businesses out of their industries. This has become a new problem which China must solve through diplomacy to maintain mutual benefit and win-win results in economic and trade relations and to make such relations the 'anchor' of China's diplomacy with big Western countries.

(2) In terms of political relations, on the one hand, China and big Western countries must continue to enhance their cooperation in the face of complicated and severe regional, international and global problems.

On the other hand, in the face of the growing discomfort, strategic anxiety and even fear on the part of major Western countries over China's peaceful but rapid development, China must take crucial steps to further develop mutual trust in its diplomacy with big Western countries.

(3) In terms of cultural exchanges, with the enhancement of China's overall national strength and the comparative decline of that of Western powers,

changing the big Western countries' sense of cultural superiority and the general mentality of Western centralism has become more important.

In addition to this, engaging Western powers in mutual exchanges and mutual learning with China and other developing countries with a more equal and more open mind on issues such as choosing the path of development or the political system have also become more important, and crucial in China's endeavors to promote global cultural diversity.

2) The Significance and Opportunity of Establishing a New Type of Big Country Relationship between China and the US

In China's overall diplomatic landscape, bilateral relations with the United States are of particular importance. It is the 'top priority' of China's foreign policy to maintain and promote the sound and steady development of China-US relations. Since the establishment of diplomatic ties over the past 30 years, despite occasional setbacks, bilateral ties have been spiraling upward with high complexity and increasing interdependence. The relationship between China and the United States weighs the most regarding their economic and social development as well as the regional and global order.

Currently, China-US relations are deepening and expanding in all directions. Their interdependence has even merged to the point of 'a bit of me in you and a bit of you in me'. In the new era when globalization, multi-polarization and informatization are developing even further, major countries cannot afford to have serious conflicts and rivalries. Both must handle it by thinking beyond the rise and fall of great powers in history and transcend the Cold War mentality between the US and the Soviet Union.

China and the US are each other's largest trading partners. Their bilateral trade volume has increased more than 220 times from less than US$2.5 billion in 1975 to US$583.7 billion in 2017. China has been America's fastest-growing export market for 10 years in a row. Bilateral mutual investment has also been expanding. By the end of 2017, two-way investment between China and the United States was over US$200 billion. Both sides have also developed profound financial interdependence. According to US Treasury data, as of July 2016, China owned about US$1.5 trillion in US Treasury bonds, which accounted for 36% of China's foreign exchange reserves and 6.2% of US treasuries, making China the largest foreign holder of US debt.

Politically, high-level contacts between the two countries have become increasingly frequent. Statistics shows that the top leaders of the two countries have met over 10 times and communicated by telephone more than 20 times since June 2013. China and the United States have established dozens of dialogue and consultation mechanisms covering almost all areas of bilateral relations, functioning as key platforms for the two sides to conduct mutual communication and policy coordination, increase mutual trust and dispel suspicion.

In terms of economic and trade relations, China and the US are already each other's second largest trading partners, with their bilateral trade volume growing by nearly 230 times from less than US$2.5 billion in the early years when China and the US established diplomatic relations to US$558.4 billion in 2015. Every day, goods and services worth over US$1.5 billion flow between the two countries. China has become the fastest growing export market for the US for 10 consecutive years. The scale of bilateral reciprocal investment is also increasing day by day. By the end of 2015, US investment in China and Chinese investment in the US had exceeded US$150 billion. The two countries have also formed a deeply interdependent relationship in finance. According to statistics revealed by the US Treasury Department, as of July 2016, China held US$1.22 trillion worth, of US Treasuries accounting for 36% of China's foreign exchange reserves and 6.2% of total US Treasuries, making China the largest foreign holder of US Treasuries. In terms of politics, the frequency of high-level contact between the two countries is unprecedented. According to statistics, from January 2009 to September 2016, top leaders of the two countries had met and talked on the phone more than 20 times respectively. Over 100 consultation and dialogue mechanisms between China and the US covering almost all aspects of their bilateral relations were established, particularly the annual strategic and economic dialogue, which has become an important platform for both sides to develop high-level communication, conduct policy coordination, enhance mutual trust and remove misgivings.

In terms of security, dialogue and cooperation between the two sides cover almost all major international and regional issues, including the management of the Korean Peninsula nuclear issue, restoring security in Afghanistan and other critical issues concerning peripheral security, as well as cooperation in non-traditional security fields such as counter-terrorism cooperation and joint maritime search and rescue operations. Despite differences and disagreements on policies and ideas between China and the US concerning security, as former US Secretary of State Hillary Clinton acknowledged: "China and the US cannot solve all the world's problems, but without China-US cooperation it is hard to solve any problem".

In terms of people-to-people, cultural and non-governmental exchanges, there are over 5 million personnel exchanges yearly in the sectors of education, science and technology and culture. By the end of 2015, nearly 600,000 Chinese people had studied in the US. Approximately 300 million Chinese people have learned or are learning English, while more than 300,000 Americans are learning Chinese as more than 1,000 American universities offer Chinese programs and over 4,000 primary and high schools open Chinese courses. The educational institutions in both countries have cooperatively established more than 100 Confucius Institutes and approximately 500 Confucius Classrooms in the US. After the China-US Governors' Forum was established, local exchanges between China and the United States have also risen to a new level. Up until now, Chinese provinces/regions/cities have developed 49 sister province/state relations and 218 sister-city relations with American states, greatly strengthening the foundation of China-US relations.

All in all, the importance of cultural and local exchanges to China-US relations are just like capillaries are to the human body. The more extensive those exchanges are, the healthier China-US relations are. On the other hand, the highs and lows of the relations accompany the developing interactions and exchanges of interest between China and the US. The differences between the two sides in terms of their political systems and ideologies frequently influence their equal dialogue on issues such as human rights. US interference in China's internal affairs on issues involving Taiwan, Tibet and the seas, hampering China's development, remains the key obstacle to strategic mutual trust between China and the United States. Since the start of the 21st century, in view of the rapid yet sustained enhancement of China's overall national strength, its more proactive approach in defending its own interests, combined with the US's relative decline in terms of overall national strength from its wars in Iraq and Afghanistan and the financial crisis, there has been an increase in domestic anxiety in the US toward China's rise to prominence, as evidenced in the calls for stronger measures to counterbalance China. Whether China and the US will repeat the 'historical tragedy' of the zero-sum game between rising powers and traditional powers is intriguing. How to overcome the 'historical tragedy' of the rise and fall of major powers has become an important question for the governments and intellectual circles of both countries.

There is no doubt that both sides should confront some persistent problems and challenges head-on and work out solutions to maintain the steady growth of China-US relations. First, the lack of strategic trust between China and the United States means both sides are likely to conjecture and analyze the other side's strategic intentions and goals from the worst-case scenario, restricting their cooperative potential. Second, US domestic factors have raised constraints on its diplomatic agenda. In particular, to manipulate domestic politics, the United States takes advantage of Taiwan and Tibet to intrude into China's internal affairs, overshadowing China's trust in the US regarding China's core interests. Third, the Asia-Pacific strategy of the US highlights the intention of its military to check against China, with sophisticated construction of regional cooperation mechanisms and the resolution of hot issues. Fourth, mutual benefits and competition in China-US bilateral trade are on the rise. Fifth, the United States still adopts a patronising attitude while negotiating with China on major international issues, fails to change the inertia of putting pressure on China, and even makes groundless accusations against China, impairing bilateral relations. Hence, it is the common historical mission for both China and the US to break down the fatalism of the rise and fall of major countries and to build a relationship featuring mutual respect and win-win cooperation.

Since November 2016 when Donald Trump was elected President of the United States, China has proactively and promptly linked up with the US governing team. Naturally, bilateral relations remained steady while the US experienced a major change in politics. The leaders of both countries visited each other within one year, and the meetings between President Xi Jinping and President Trump at Mar-a-Lago resort and in Beijing achieved significant results. China and the United States agreed to give further strategic guidance to the China-US relationship through presidential diplomacy. The two countries have strengthened exchanges at the top and other levels by means of the four high-level dialogue mechanisms of China-US diplomatic security, comprehensive economy, society and humanity, and law enforcement and cyber security. They have a consensus to expand cooperation in a wide range of areas on the basis of mutual benefit, to manage differences on the basis of mutual respect, to strengthen mutual understanding and friendship between the two peoples, and to jointly address major international and regional issues and global challenges.

Despite the overall stability and progress after the new American government came into office, China-US relations are still faced with new difficulties and uncertainties. First, US domestic strategic anxieties and misgivings about China's rise are on the increase. The Trump administration recently released its *National Security Strategy* (2017), in which China is regarded as a major strategic competitor of the United States. Meanwhile, it exaggerates the 'Failure of America's Policy of Engagement with China' and propagates a 'Coercive Strategy via Strength', and is scheming the so-called 'Indo-Pacific Strategy' against China. Second, the Trump Administration prioritizes US interests with the implementation of its 'America First' foreign policy. On trade and economic issues with China, the US, with disregard for the multilateral trade rules such as the WTO, is suppressing normal cooperation between Chinese and American technology enterprises through non-market means, leading to more China-US trade and economic spats, or even conflicts. Third, some within the Trump Administration are trying to continue the manipulation of the Taiwan strait, the South China sea, the Korean nuclear and other issues to keep China in check and under pressure. In brief, at the new historical stage, China-US relations harbor opportunities for further development and confront instabilities and uncertainties. Nevertheless, as long as they both maintain a strategic consensus of broad common interests and important responsibilities in safeguarding world peace, stability and prosperity, continue to expand cooperation in all areas on the basis of mutual benefit and reciprocity, properly manage differences and disagreements on the basis of mutual respect, strengthen mutual understanding and friendship between the two peoples, and jointly address major regional and global challenges, China and the US can keep promoting the sustained and stable development of China-US relations.

3) The Significance and Prospects of Building a Comprehensive China-EU Strategic Partnership

From China's point of view, Europe is a set of amalgamated concepts with the dual attributes of geography and politics, representing not only various institutions in Europe (the EU) and the governments of nation states that constitute the EU, but also those countries which have not joined the EU but are still part of Europe geographically. For this reason, China's relations and diplomacy with Europe and the EU are structurally asymmetrical and comprise a mix of bilateralism and multilateralism, leading to more complexity, diversity and richness compared to relations with other big countries. Since the 1990s the China-EU relationship has been developing at unprecedented speed. In 1998, China and the EU were committed to building a long-term, stable, and constructive partnership for the 21st century. In 2001, the two sides decided to build a comprehensive partnership. In 2003, they decided to develop a comprehensive strategic partnership. Due to the differences in historical tradition, political system, ideology and economic development level, the China-EU relationship has faced all kinds of obstacles along the way but, in general, it has become one of the most stable, influential and constructive models of big country relations in the world. What are the motives behind the comprehensive China-EU strategic partnership and what are its prospects?

First and foremost, high-level officials on both sides have a positive perception of the importance of developing the comprehensive China-EU strategic partnership in the new era to both partners and globally. Although China and the EU have different understandings of what constitutes the comprehensive strategic partnership, both sides endorse the view that there are no fundamental strategic conflicts of interests between China and the EU in comparison with other major countries. 'A tighter, stronger strategic partnership suits the interests of both the EU and China'. Comparatively speaking, the Chinese government has a clearer and deeper understanding of promoting the China-EU comprehensive strategic partnership. In May 2004, then-Premier Wen Jiabao delivered a speech entitled *Actively Developing the Comprehensive China-EU Strategic Partnership* in Brussels, in which he pointed out that the term 'comprehensive' suggests an all-round, wide-ranging and multi-level cooperation between the two sides, not only in terms of economics and technology, but also politics and culture, which is also both bilateral and multilateral; and both governmental and non-governmental. The term 'strategic' suggests overall, long-term and stable cooperation which, despite differences in ideology and social systems, is not susceptible to disturbance by any isolated incident. The term 'partnership' suggests equal, altruistic and win-win cooperation, based on mutual respect and trust, which seeks consensus on major issues while reserving differences on minor issues and endeavors to expand the common interests of both sides. Moreover, China believes that the comprehensive China-EU strategic partnership is characterized by 'growth' and 'inclusiveness', meaning that the China-EU relationship is capable of adapting to the changing environment. The two sides can together make a serious appraisal of the overall situation, tolerate differences and defuse frictions.

Second, the increasingly close economic and trade ties between China and the EU, as well as cooperation in other fields, have become the cornerstone of the comprehensive China-EU strategic partnership. Bilateral trade between China and the EU increased from US$40.3 billion in 1995 to US$86.8 billion in 2002. It continued to grow rapidly over the following decade, maintaining an annual growth rate of 20% to 40%, except in 2009 when the impact of the financial crisis led to a decline. Since the financial crisis in 2008, both sides have worked actively to reduce its impact on bilateral trade and to realize a quick trade rebound with a growth rate of 32% in 2010. The growth rate reached 18.3% in 2011 with a total trade volume of US$567.21 billion. Bilateral trade remained high at US$546 billion in 2012 in spite of the continued effects of the European debt crisis. The EU has remained China's largest trade partner for nine consecutive years, and China has become the EU's second largest trade partner. Mutual investment between China and the EU has continued to grow. By the end of 2012, the EU had a total of 36,639 direct investment projects in China with an actual investment portfolio of US$83.93 billion. In 2012, the EU had 1,698 direct investment projects in China, and the actual investment portfolio was US$6.11 billion. In the same year, Chinese non-financial investment in Europe was US$3.41 billion. Over the past few years, China has continued to increase its investment in the EU, and Europe has become China's largest area of investment. On May 24, 2013, China signed a bilateral free trade agreement with Switzerland - the first free trade agreement China has signed with a continental European country and one of the world's 20 leading economies. It has had a strong demonstrative effect, promoting the upgrading of China-Europe trade and investment.

Moreover, ever since the European sovereign debt crisis, China has adhered to an approach to the European situation that complements the general direction of the EU's development as well as its socio-economic principles. China has constantly attached great importance to its relations with the EU from a strategic and long-term perspective, actively projecting confidence in Europe and European integration. It has spared no effort in providing help to the EU through bilateral and multilateral channels. When the EU was in distress, China did not predict its decline but remained optimistic about its future, actively supporting the former's efforts to overcome its plight. China and the EU not only actively sent positive signals of cooperation to the international community through multilateral platforms such as the G20, which stabilized the confidence of the international market, but also presented a positive attitude by providing a capital increase of US$4.3 billion to the International Monetary Fund (IMF), helping the EU with practical actions to overcome the sovereign debt crisis and enjoy an earlier economic recovery.

Third are the official consultation and communication mechanisms between China and the EU at various levels, as well as growing cultural exchanges playing the important roles of 'stabilizer' and 'pressure reducer', which have strengthened mutual trust and relieved tension. The annual China-EU Summit is the highest political dialogue mechanism. Established in 1998, it has been held 16 times. The China-EU High-level Strategic Dialogue is an important platform for China and the EU to have in-depth communication on macro strategic issues. So far, four rounds of the dialogue have been held. The two sides have not only maintained close high-level political interaction but have also set up over 60 dialogue and consultation mechanisms, covering fields such as politics, economy, trade, culture, technology, energy and the environment. In recent years, China's big country cooperation and sub-regional cooperation with Europe have reached a new, higher level, which has greatly enriched China-EU relations. China and Germany held two rounds of political consultations, which set a precedent for such mechanisms between China and a big Western country. China and France have scored remarkable achievements of cooperation in fields such as aviation, nuclear energy and low-carbon energy. China and the UK have made progress in cooperation concerning infrastructure and investment. In 2012, Chinese leaders successfully met with the leaders of 16 countries in Central and Eastern Europe, which is another important innovation in the form and content of China-EU cooperation.

In the second decade of the new millennium, China is further promoting a new type of partnership of comprehensive cooperation and common prosperity with the EU based on mutual respect and learning. China emphasizes the importance of transcending differences in ideology and social systems and the zero-sum mentality of 'winning and losing'. All in all, China and the EU are two major forces in the globalization of the world economy, and the strategic and overall significance of China-EU relations will further increase.

4) Prospects and Challenges of Building Strategic China-Japan Reciprocal Relations

It has always been an integral part of modern China's diplomacy to properly manage its relations with Japan. China and Japan are close neighbors facing each other across a narrow strip of water. Over almost 2,000 years, there has not only been a long history of friendly interaction, with the strong (China) helping the weak (Japan), but also a more recent stage when Japan bullied and invaded China, who bravely resisted. In September 1972, Japanese Prime Minister Kakuei Tanaka visited China, and the two sides issued the *China-Japan Joint Communiqué*, announcing the establishment of diplomatic ties. Since the signing of the *China-Japan Treaty of Peace and Friendship* in August 1978, the two sides have begun to develop their relations on equal terms.

From the Chinese perspective, after over 40 years of developing its diplomacy with Japan, bilateral exchanges in every field have reached unprecedented breadth and depth, laying a solid foundation for the further expansion of bilateral relations. In terms of politics, China and Japan have signed four political documents successively, namely the *China-Japan Joint Communiqué*, the *China-Japan Treaty of Peace and Friendship*, the *China-Japan Joint Declaration* and the *Joint Statement on the All-Round Promotion of China-Japan Strategic Reciprocal Relations*, which have become the political principles guiding the stable and healthy development of China-Japan relations.

Economic interdependence and cooperation between China and Japan have continued to deepen. On the one hand, Japan's capital, technology and managerial expertise have supported the process of China's reform and opening up. On the other hand, China's vast market has also provided Japan with great opportunities and resources for its industrial transfer, restructuring and development. China has now become Japan's largest trade partner and Japan, in turn, is China's second largest trade partner and largest foreign investor. Since the financial crisis, China and Japan have enhanced their economic and trade cooperation, which has enabled both parties to resist the impact of the global economic crisis and accelerate the pace of their economic recovery. In addition, bilateral trade has partly achieved direct trading between the Chinese Rmb and the Japanese yen, indicating substantial progress in terms of financial cooperation. Cultural exchanges between China and Japan have made great advances. Personnel exchanges went up from 10,000 people per year 40 years ago to currently over 5 million per year, and there are as many as 250 sister province/county/city relationships. Almost 100 flights carrying approximately 18,000 people travel between China and Japan daily. All in all, stable and healthy China-Japan relations not only suit the interests of both countries, but also benefit the prosperity and stability of the entire Asia-Pacific region and even the whole world. Based on strategic considerations on developing bilateral relations between China and Japan, the Chinese and Japanese governments signed the *Joint Statement on the All-Round Promotion of China-Japan Strategic Reciprocal Relations* in 2008, confirming that 'long-term peace, friendship and cooperation is the only choice for the two sides. China and Japan are committed to the all-round promotion of strategic reciprocal relations in order to realize the goals of peaceful coexistence, friendship for generations, mutually beneficial cooperation and common development between China and Japan'.

What cannot be denied is that modern China's diplomacy with Japan over the last 40 years has been full of ups and downs, and twists and turns. A series of problems surfacing from Japan have disrupted if not damaged the development of China-Japan relations. In summary, there are three major problems as follows.

The first problem concerns territorial disputes, with the current focus on the Diaoyu Islands. The root of the Diaoyu Islands issue is that Japan illegitimately occupied Chinese territory. As China and Japan were normalizing relations and concluding the *China-Japan Treaty of Peace and Friendship* in the 1970s, the then-leaders of the two countries, acting in the larger interest of China-Japan relations, reached an important understanding and consensus to 'leave the issue of the Diaoyu Islands to be resolved later'. However, in recent years, due to the determination of Japanese right-wing conservative forces to expand their maritime territorial rights, Japan has ignored this history and denies China's sovereignty over the Diaoyu Islands. This has become the political mainstream in Japan. On September 10, 2012, the Japanese government announced the 'purchase' of the Diaoyu Islands and the accompanying south and north islands, continuing its so-called 'nationalization' regardless of China's resistance. Evidently, this is not only a serious violation of China's territorial sovereignty, a severe blow to 1.3 billion Chinese people and a gross violation of historical facts and international law, but also a public rejection of the victory of the World Anti-Fascist War and a serious challenge to the post-war international order. The Japanese government's position is inevitably met with firm opposition and strong protest from the Chinese government and people, and therefore China-Japan relations are seriously worsening.

The second problem regards historical issues, particularly the Yasukuni

Shrine issue, which has hit a sensitive nerve for China. Japanese politicians visiting a shrine that whitewashes Japan's wartime aggression and honors 14 Class A war criminals - including Hideki Tojo - is no doubt a subversion of Japan's history of aggression in the Second World War and a grave injury to the feelings of victims in the affected countries. In terms of its relations with Japan, China adheres to the principle of 'using history as a mirror to look into the future', which means that only when the Japanese government reflects on its history in a genuine and responsible manner and thoroughly breaks away from its militarism through practical actions can it build a bright future together with East Asian countries including China. Ever since the normalization of China-Japan diplomatic relations, when the Japanese government took the right position, the development of its relationship with China has been smoother, but when it does not, it damages this relationship. However, the Japanese government's recognition of, and position concerning, historical issues often changes. Since the 21st century, encouraged by Japanese right-wing conservative forces, voices that ignore history and even attempt to cover up its history of aggression continue to arise in the Japanese government. Towards the end of 2012, Shinzo Abe, the spokesperson of Japanese conservative forces, took office. The Japanese government's recognition of its actions during the Second World War again dramatically changed, seriously affecting political trust between China and Japan.

The third problem concerns the Taiwan issue. Although the Japanese government recognizes the government of the PRC as the sole legal government, it is reluctant to explicitly recognize Taiwan as part of China. Japan hopes that this will enable it to retain its influence over the Taiwan issue and Cross-Strait relations. The Taiwan issue remains important in China-Japan relations. The three structural problems in China-Japan relations mentioned above have historical roots, but the extent of their disruption to the health and stability of the relationship is closely related to the fact that Japanese right-wing conservative forces have continued to gain momentum since the 21st century. After its economic bubble burst in the 1990s, Japan plunged into a long economic slump which, coupled with its declining birth rate, ageing population and long-term political instability, increased disillusionment and anxiety in Japanese society. At the same time, China's overall national strength rapidly increased, resulting in a 'reversal of the century' in its balance of power with Japan, which Japan did not anticipate. Japanese right-wing conservative forces took the opportunity to promote the image of China as a 'threat', stressing that Japan's mainstream ideological trend includes 'New Nationalism' which proposes building Japan's power by strengthening the US-Japan military alliance. It has become an ideological barrier disrupting and affecting the development of China-Japan strategic reciprocal relations.

Therefore, in order to resolve the negative factors affecting China-Japan relations and promote the building of a mutually beneficial China-Japan strategic relationship China - and especially Japan - must continue to earnestly implement the following principles. First, they must approach the development of China-Japan relations from a strategic level and with a general perspective. Only when both sides are fully committed to the idea that long-term friendship and cooperation between China and Japan is the only choice for both countries, can both governments gather their political will to safeguard the development of bilateral relations and jointly resolve factors that disrupt and sabotage it. This is particularly crucial for the Japanese government. Second, they must stick faithfully to their political commitments. Building China-Japan 'reciprocal and cooperative relations based on common strategic interests' is an inevitable choice, but the crux is how to promote the development of a mutually beneficial China-Japan strategic relationship, making the relationship not only written on government documents but also implemented by concrete actions of both countries. The core is that the Japanese government should abandon its zero-sum mentality, and consider China's development an opportunity instead of a threat. Japan should keep expanding its common interests with China through deepening cooperation, and increase the strategic mutual trust with China with practical actions. Third, they must pay attention to the overall interests and manage crises promptly. China stresses that there are both historical disputes and actual conflicts between China and Japan, many of which, like the territorial disputes, are highly complex and sensitive and which, if handled without discretion, can cause clashes of public opinion in both countries, or even severely impact bilateral relations. For this reason, whether Japan can adhere to the principles and norms of the four political documents both governments have signed, prevent regressive acts being committed by its domestic right-wing conservative forces and safeguard the overall interests of China-Japan relations is another key factor in the future development of China-Japan reciprocal relations.

II. The Development of China's Diplomacy with Emerging Powers (BRICS)

1) Elevation of Strategic Positioning

Emerging powers are not included in China's traditional major country diplomacy, and until recently China was not aware of the concept of emerging powers. From its reform and opening up to the 1990s, China developed its relations with India, Brazil, Russia and South Africa from a bilateral and regional perspective, and considered them developing or transitional countries in a broad sense. In the 21st century, China is paying increasing attention to these promising countries with emerging market economies, and is ensuring that China's big country diplomacy includes emerging powers, and particularly the BRICS countries[1], which account for 40% of the world population, 26% of the planet's land area, and 23% (and rising) of the global economy.

The extent to which China elevates the strategic positioning of emerging powers through its diplomacy depends on its deep insight into three historical factors and how they serve the rise of these powers. These three factors have not only made the collective rise of emerging powers a reality, but have also made cooperative mechanisms between them possible.

First, a common feature of emerging powers is their shared ability to exert a pulling effect on economic globalization based on their own situations and through internal institutional reform, as well as their ability to emulate and innovate. As a result they have become the frontrunners in catching up with developed Western economies. This has become their shared 'international identity' despite their differences in terms of historical tradition, social system and development path.

Second, the collective rise of emerging powers has taken place in a historical context in which the international agenda has witnessed major historical changes. On the one hand, like other members of the international community, emerging powers face the challenges of transnational and

---

1. The BRICs first referred to four promising emerging-market countries, namely Brazil, Russia, India and China. The term was first coined by American economist Jim O'Neill of Goldman Sachs in December 2001. He used the initials of Brazil, Russia, India and China to form the acronym, which is pronounced the same as 'brick'. In December 2010, the four countries agreed to formally include South Africa in the mechanism, resulting in the name BRICS with the capital 'S' standing for South Africa.

global issues with increasing severity and complexity. The policy agenda of emerging powers in the 21st century includes major issues ranging from promoting sustainable and inclusive development to dealing with 'nexus security' stemming from the interaction and integration of issues like water resources, land resources, food security, energy security and climate change. On the other hand, emerging powers have transformed from passively receiving and handling non-traditional development and security issues in the past to actively participating in the proposal, guidance and even design of the transnational and global agenda. Whether they are in areas such as global climate change, world trade negotiations or reforming the current international financial system, emerging powers are playing a much more active role.

Last, strengthening the cooperative mechanisms among emerging powers is also the result of a 'collective response' to new issues and challenges of global and national governance. In order to promote the reform and construction of current global governance mechanisms in terms of economy, politics, development and security and make them more legitimate and effective, emerging powers must coordinate their positions and cooperate with each other. In the face of increasingly complex domestic tasks of development and governance, emerging powers must continue to communicate and share their experiences in development, and jointly respond to problems such as the 'middle-income trap' that they commonly face.

All in all, emerging powers have become an increasingly important part of China's big country diplomacy, not only because of their positive development prospects and increasing influence, but also because of the fact that their new common identity, common roles, common tasks and common interests have created plenty of room for them to strengthen their cooperative mechanisms and become an increasingly significant collective force arising in a new era of international relations.

2) Promoting Transformation and Upgrading of the Global Governance System

In the new century, China has not only continued to strengthen its bilateral relations with emerging powers, and especially with the BRICS countries, but it has also established a platform of collective cooperation with them, which has become the greatest achievement and most recent symbol of China's diplomacy with emerging powers. The establishment of a cooperative platform with the BRICS countries in particular has created a new opportunity to further strengthen the initiative and ability of emerging powers to coordinate and cooperate with each other in transforming and upgrading the global governance system. This is evident in the following aspects.

First, emerging powers have accelerated the process of global multi-polarization and filled the asymmetrical gaps between the global North and South in international institutions. Since the end of the Second World War, the asymmetry in the relationship between the North and South in global governance has become evident. As a club of developed Western economies, the G7 has remained at the core of the global economic governance system for too long, and the interaction between developed countries has influenced and determined the face and trend of the global economic landscape to a great extent. For countries of the global South, on the other hand, besides the loosely-knit Group of 77, an organization or mechanism that can match the power bloc of developed countries in a real sense is lacking. Even then, the Group of 77 has underachieved in the global economy. This situation has changed in the 21st century, especially in recent years as the BRICS countries have emphasized strengthening coordination and cooperation, which have become the core of emerging powers' cooperative mechanisms. Since 2009, the BRICS Summit has become regularized and institutionalized as one of the most important platforms for emerging economies to cooperate with each other. The establishment and continued improvement of cooperative mechanisms between emerging powers has also provided more institutionalized platforms for them to coordinate their positions in international multilateral organizations such as the UN, Group of 20 (G20), International Monetary Fund (IMF) and the World Bank, and to increase the collective influence of emerging powers at international multilateral events. One significant result is that by 2011, the percentage of the total votes of developing countries in the World Bank had risen from 44.06% to 47.19%, and the percentage of votes in the IMF had risen from 40.5% to 42.1%. In 2016, China, while shouldering its G20 presidency, enabled the IMF to put long-delayed reforms into action with the help of other emerging great powers and developing countries. Hence, countries of both the South and North can have more of an equal influence in global economic decision-making, and the global governance mechanism can become more reasonable and balanced.

Second, emerging powers have become the new engine of economic globalization, and have propelled industrial civilization and modernization into a new era. One common feature of the collective rise of emerging powers is that they have all seized opportunities presented by economic globalization, actively implemented internal reform and tapped into the resource allocation of the global market while unleashing their own economic potential, and enriching and diversifying the connotation of globalization. In the context of the continued intensification of the financial crisis of 2008 and the European debt crisis of 2011, out of concern for their domestic economic interests, developed Western countries erected all kinds of investment and trade protectionist measures under various pretexts such as national security, environmental protection and fair competition, hindering the further opening of global trade and investment to various degrees. Emerging powers are both the beneficiaries of globalization and committed defenders of the open market economy. While strengthening their cooperation, emerging powers are striving to make the further promotion of the opening of global trade and investment an important policy agenda in order to inject new impetus into economic globalization. From a broader historical perspective, the rise of emerging powers is a historical result of the spread of modernization, which is represented by Western industrial civilization, to a global scope. However, due to differences in historical context and the scale of their rise, the industrialization and modernization of emerging powers cannot replicate the Western model of aggression, plunder and colonization. Emerging powers are making efforts to explore a model of growth through peace, cooperation, mutual benefit and win-win results. This practice of peaceful growth is in itself likely to bring the benefits of modernization to more people and more regions, and by doing so lift the traditional industrial civilization and modernization led by the West to a higher level.

Last, emerging powers have boosted and become a new constructive force in the institutional reform of global governance. On the one hand, faced with lack of representation within the global governance mechanism, emerging powers contributed to its reform and reconstruction, and their roles are transforming from general participants to constructive contributors. In areas such as global trade, energy security, financial cooperation, international development and investment promotion, emerging powers are playing a more central role. For example, in light of the impact of the volatility of international financial capital on emerging markets after the financial crisis, the 2012 BRICS Summit in New Delhi proposed the establishment of the 'BRICS New Development Bank', which received general support from the BRICS governments and various financial institutions. Up until now, the BRICS countries have officially established a new development bank, emergency reserve arrangement and other mechanisms, all in smooth operation. On the other hand, the deficiency and incompetence of the Western-dominated regulatory concepts and mechanisms in the face of the challenges of globalization allowed the international community to begin searching for a new path and learn from past experiences, particularly after the financial crisis and the European debt crisis, when Western countries themselves experienced institutional dilemmas such as under-regulated financial capital, an imbalance between the virtual and the real economy, the unsustainability of elaborate welfare systems, an increasing divide between rich and poor, and political instability caused by partisanship. The contribution of emerging powers to global governance not only lies in the fact that they are gradually driving the engine of global economic growth, but is also found in their historical heritages and cultural values which, unfortunately, have been underestimated for too long. The spirit and qualities of learning, innovation, reform and autonomy demonstrated by emerging powers in the process of economic globalization are providing new diversified plans for the development of global governance.

3) Focus of China's Diplomacy with Emerging Powers

First, it has been an important part of China's diplomacy with emerging powers from the beginning to form a cohesive strategic level of cooperation, and in particular to jointly explore and shape a forward-looking and inclusive outlook on the international system. For example, in developing its relations with Russia, China stresses that 'based on their common ground on major international issues, the two sides pay great attention to creating a positive agenda that brings all parties together in international relations, in order to jointly respond to current challenges and ensure sustainable social and economic development'. The *Delhi Declaration* ratified at the 2012 BRICS Summit states that 'the BRICS countries are a platform of dialogue and cooperation for promoting peace, security and development in a world of multi-polarization, interdependence, increasing complexity and globalization. We come from Asia, Africa, Europe and Latin America, and the transcontinental nature of our interaction adds value and significance to our cooperation'. The statement further indicates the consciousness and confidence of the BRICS countries to push the development of the international system and order towards a more just and reasonable direction through strengthening collective cooperation. It is safe to say that with the deepening of the multi-polarization of international forces, emerging powers can and should make the development of common interests and values their goal, and on this basis form a new international system and order with other major actors.

Next, deepening institutional cooperation between emerging powers has become another important task in China's diplomacy. All emerging powers, including China, have reached a point where they need institutional guarantees for their own global interests. Cooperation between emerging powers not only increases the ability to fend off external risks for every country involved, but also produces the overall effect of '1+1>2' through safeguarding their own interests and pushing for reform of the international system. At present, China has not only established strategic partnerships in various forms with all emerging powers, but it has also strived for institutional cooperation between emerging powers, and in particular the BRICS countries. The continuous and regularized convening of the BRICS Summits since the Yekaterinburg Summit has become a significant symbol of this process of institutionalization. Currently, the cooperative mechanisms between the BRICS countries have gradually become multi-level platforms which include meetings between leaders, meetings between senior representatives for security issues, meetings between foreign ministers, ministerial meetings and meetings between coordinators. The mechanisms also involve occasional communication between envoys in multilateral organizations and pragmatic cooperation in various areas, which is combined with an expanding and developing non-governmental cooperative network including the BRICS Think Tank Council, the annual BRICS inter-bank cooperation mechanism meeting and financial forum, and the BRICS Business Council as well as other growing non-governmental cooperative networks. At the same time, China's bilateral and multilateral pragmatic cooperation with the BRICS countries is also increasing, and the high value and cohesion of this cooperation fits the metaphor of 'gold bricks' (a play on the Chinese word for BRICS, *jinzhuan*, which literally means gold brick). Although formal organizational mechanisms such as a secretariat have not yet been established, the cooperative mechanisms between the BRICS countries adhere to the principles of transparency, solidarity, deepening cooperation and seeking common development. These are the main themes of current affairs and therefore fit the expectations of the international community.

Finally, it should not be ignored that besides the great potential for cooperation between the emerging powers, properly managing their internal disagreements and strengthening their ability to respond to external challenges are priorities in China's diplomacy with emerging powers. The current challenges are twofold. On the one hand, emerging powers are still at a primary stage and there are various differences and disagreements between them. For example, on the issue of reforming the UN Security Council (UNSC), strong agreements exist between the current permanent members of the UNSC and those inclined to become permanent members. In terms of trans-regional cooperation, the attempt of India, Brazil and South Africa to represent Asia, Africa and Latin America with a three-country mechanism was questioned by other emerging powers. Another example concerns the values of the international system. China and Russia differ greatly from India, Brazil and Mexico in their prioritization of 'freedom, democracy and human rights'. In terms of regional (or sub-regional) cooperation, China and Russia also have different ideas and practices to India, Mexico and Brazil. There are also conflicts of interest between emerging powers, which can sometimes even lead to public disputes. Most importantly, serious defects exist in the internal structure of emerging powers, including the BRICS countries. They bear features of developing countries and transitional economies, and have questionable structural quality and sustainability in terms of their economic and social structures, as well as their governmental structures. Emerging powers have, however, become aware of the importance of resolving internal disagreements and the structural challenges of their own development. They are striving to form common interests that transcend their differences through expanding multilateral interactions and reaching compromises.

On the other hand, China must at the same time properly manage its relations with traditional Western powers and other developing countries. To emerging powers, traditional Western powers are the original rule makers and fierce defenders of the current order. They are, to various degrees, structural competitors to emerging powers in terms of their interactions. At the same time, in an era of economic interdependence and close security links, traditional Western powers are also important partners with whom emerging powers must cooperate. This complex 'co-opertition' requires emerging powers to gradually attain the status that matches their strength and institutional rights and become constructive stakeholders of the international community and positive contributors to the new international order. They must achieve this through changing dynamics with traditional Western powers under the current institutional framework, and incremental reform. At the same time, as the frontrunners of developing countries, emerging powers inevitably face differences and even conflicts with other developing countries in terms of their interests and priorities. If emerging powers want to retain their special roles in the evolution of the international system, they should strive to become contributors and leaders who help more developing countries to realize sustainable development, instead of 'the international new upstarts' who are disconnected with developing countries' interests, concerns and identities.

4) Significance and Prospects of Deepening China-Russia Comprehensive Strategic Partnership of Coordination

The China-Russia strategic partnership of coordination can be dated back to as early as 1996 when former Russian President Yeltsin visited China. Both sides signed *The Joint China-Russia Statement,* and promised to jointly build "a strategic partnership of coordination of equality and mutual trust oriented towards the 21st century". In the following decade, the China-Russia comprehensive strategic partnership of coordination has been enriched continuously. In 2011, which marked the 10th anniversary of the signing of the *China-Russian Treaty of Good-Neighborliness, Friendship and Cooperation*, the two countries declared their intention to develop a comprehensive partnership of coordination based on equality and mutual trust, mutual support, common prosperity and lasting friendship. From 2013 to 2016, Chinese President Xi Jinping and Russian President Vladimir Putin frequently made exchange visits. The two sides stressed that China and Russia should stick to the spirit of strategic cooperation and the concept of lasting friendship, increase mutual support, promote political and strategic mutual trust, and unswervingly deepen the China-Russia comprehensive strategic partnership of coordination. With the joint efforts of the two countries, the China-Russia comprehensive strategic partnership of coordination always keeps running at a high level, playing an important role in maintaining international and regional peace and stability.

The China-Russia comprehensive strategic partnership of coordination is based on the Five Principles of Peaceful Coexistence. It's a new type of state relations featuring non-alliance, non-confrontation, and not being against any third country. The establishment of the strategic partnership has created conditions for the two sides to conduct the most extensive and mutually beneficial cooperation in all fields. With this partnership, China and Russia enjoy political equality, mutually beneficial cooperation in economy, mutual trust in security, and enhanced coordination in international affairs.

First, the foundation of the China-Russia comprehensive strategic partnership of coordination is to develop bilateral relations so as to maintain everlasting, good-neighborly and friendly relations, to promote the common development and prosperity of both countries, and to benefit the peoples of both countries. Next, the strategic partnership requires both to closely consult and coordinate in international affairs to safeguard their own independence, sovereignty, national dignity, due status in the international community and legitimate rights and interests. Finally, through bilateral cooperation and concerted efforts, the strategic partnership is meant to alleviate tension, enhance stability, and mobilize the world towards multi-polarization and facilitate the establishment of a new international order that is fair and just.

The China-Russia comprehensive strategic partnership of coordination covers the following major areas:

First, political coordination. Within the framework of the comprehensive strategic partnership of coordination, China and Russia have set up regular meeting mechanisms of presidents, foreign ministers and of different government levels and professional fields to continuously strengthen mutual trust and cooperation in politics. China and Russia have reached extensive consensus on safeguarding national sovereignty and territorial integrity, opposing interference in each other's internal affairs, upholding the diversity of civilizations, and respecting the development paths chosen by each country. The two countries support each other and continuously promote coordination in the political field.

Second, diplomatic coordination. Within the framework of the comprehensive strategic partnership of coordination, China and Russia have acted in concert and actively coordinate with each other in diplomatic strategy. The two countries are committed to opposing hegemonism and power politics, pushing for the establishment of a more reasonable international political and economic order, and insisting on safeguarding the UN's authority. At the regional level, China and Russia have co-founded the SCO, maintained the security and stability of the Eurasia inland area, jointly promoted the development of a diverse and equal regional security system, and actively conducted cooperation in multilateral mechanisms such as the G20, APEC and BRICS. The two countries have also closely worked together to impel peaceful resolutions to such hot security issues as the Korean Peninsula nuclear issue, the Iranian nuclear issue and the Syria crisis, so as to maintain the enduring peace and stability of this region.

Third, military technology cooperation. Within the framework of the comprehensive strategic partnership of coordination, China and Russia have actively carried out military and technology cooperation. Since the 1990s, China has been the biggest importer of Russia's weaponry, building a solid foundation for China's modernization in military technology. China has bought from Russia Su-27, Su-30 and Su-35 fighters, Type-956 destroyers, Kilo-class conventional diesel submarines, S300 and S400 anti-aircraft missile systems, and key aero-engine parts. These have laid a solid foundation for the modernization of China's military technology. On the other hand, China's orders have provided Russian military enterprises, which were in the midst of transformation, with the money they need for further transformation and development. In addition, the Chinese and Russian armies have also carried out dialogue, joint military exercises and exchange visits of various kinds.

Fourth, energy cooperation. China and Russia are important energy partners. The China-Russia crude oil pipeline was put into commercial operation in January 2011. The China-Russia east line natural gas pipeline construction project was launched successively with the section in Russia in September 2014 and that in China in June 2015. Russia is always among China's top three sources of petroleum imports. In addition, the two countries' energy enterprises have conducted extensive cooperation in jointly developing oil and gas resources, nuclear energy and coal.

Fifth, economic and trade cooperation. Great potential exists in the economic and trade cooperation of China and Russia. After the establishment of the China-Russia comprehensive strategic partnership of coordination, the volume of bilateral trade soared, peaking in 2014 at US$95.28 billion. Since 2011, China has become Russia's largest trading partner, and there's still great potential and broad prospects in economic and trade cooperation between the two sides. The governments of both sides focus on implementing strategic cooperative projects, positively promoting the improvement of the two countries' trade structure, trying to extend bilateral trade in emerging fields, and encouraging Chinese and Russian enterprises to conduct cross-border investment, so as to achieve the goal of bilateral trade between the two sides reaching US$200 billion by 2020.

Sixth, people-to-people exchanges and cooperation. Within the framework of the China-Russia comprehensive strategic partnership of coordination, cultural collaboration between the two countries has blossomed. The two countries have hosted national-level thematic year activities including national year, year of language, year of tourism, year of friendly exchanges of the youth and year of media exchanges, which have improved mutual understanding of the people of both countries and consolidated their traditional friendship. At the same time, the two sides have also committed to strengthening the 'Track II' strategic dialogue mechanism which complements exchanges between the two governments with exchanges between the two countries' academia, to promote the sense of cooperation between the two sides.

With more than 20 years' practice, the China-Russia comprehensive strategic partnership of coordination has stepped onto a new stage of steady development. The partnership has become an effective strategic model of friendly coordination between countries under new circumstances, and offers the international community a good model of state-to-state relations. The China-Russia comprehensive strategic partnership of coordination enjoys very broad future development prospects.

First, China and Russia will constantly deepen and extend their strategic coordination, and promote sustainable and steady development of bilateral cooperation. Led by the China-Russia comprehensive strategic partnership of coordination, the two sides' cooperation in all areas has been strongly advanced. Cooperation in politics, diplomacy, military and energy has reached a high strategic level, while cooperation in other fields has also shown enormous potential. The China-Russia comprehensive strategic partnership of coordination has laid a solid foundation for good-neighborliness and long-term cooperation between the two countries.

Second, the China-Russia comprehensive strategic partnership of coordination will further promote the peace, stability and development of Eurasia. The stable development of China-Russia relations has exerted a positive influence on Eurasia, especially Central Asia. After the establishment of the China-Russia comprehensive strategic partnership of coordination, the border areas of China, Russia and Central Asian countries have cultivated a new environment of steady peace. These countries have reduced their military deployment by large amounts and put more resources into economic construction. Meanwhile, the increase in mutual trust among these countries has continuously strengthened economic ties among them, and has provided favorable conditions for regional stability and development.

Third, as a pioneering model of bilateral relations, comprehensive strategic coordination won't make the two countries allied. Drawing on the experience and lessons from the long historical interactions between the two countries, China and Russia forged this comprehensive strategic partnership of coordination, a relationship model of historic significance and pertinent to reality. This partnership is strategic, non-ideological and not against any third country, and is based on the premise of the two countries' common interests and development goals. It's a special model of exchanges, conforming to the principles of state law, under which the bilateral relations won't move towards a traditional military alliance. The China-Russia comprehensive strategic partnership of coordination will last for a long time and continue to increase in scale and influence, promoting the sustainable and stable development of China-Russia relations.

Finally, the Belt and Road initiative will play an important role in the China-Russia strategic partnership of coordination in the future. After President Xi Jinping proposed the idea of a 'Silk Road Economic Belt' in 2013, jointly building the Silk Road Economic Belt has become an important topic in China-Russia relations. In May 2015, heads of China and Russia endorsed and issued the *China-Russia Joint Statement on Docking of the Silk Road Economic Belt Initiative and the EAEU Construction*, marking the official start of the two sides' Eurasian economic cooperation. The two countries will focus on issues related to the Belt and Road initiative to conduct cooperation and construction, so as to inject new impetus into the development of the China-Russia comprehensive strategic partnership of coordination. It's estimated that for a long period of time to come, the Belt and Road initiative will play an important role in the construction and development of the China-Russia comprehensive strategic partnership of coordination.

(By Chen Dongxiao)

Chapter 4

China's Diplomacy with Other Developing Countries

The foundation of China's diplomacy rests on its relations with other developing countries. Even though its meaning and aims vary with the times, the theme running through China's diplomacy with other developing countries is development. From the 1960s to the 1970s, China and other developing countries experienced anti-imperialist, anti-colonial and anti-hegemony struggles. During this time China and other developing countries shared the common goal of realizing the independent development of their nations. From the 1980s to the 1990s, with the implementation of its reform and opening up, the focus of China's diplomacy with other developing countries was gradually shifted to comprehensive cooperation guided by the principles of equality and mutual benefit. The major goals of China's diplomacy with other developing countries in this phase were realizing common development and narrowing the gap between the developing and developed countries. With the collective rise of emerging markets at the beginning of the 21st century, the international order has experienced changes which have presented both new challenges and a new era for the diplomacy of China and other developing countries. The construction of a more equitable and reasonable global governance mechanism and the promotion of peace and development have therefore become the major goals of China's diplomacy with other developing countries.

I. Principal Concepts of China's Diplomacy with Other Developing Countries

In short, the principal concepts of China's diplomacy with other developing countries are equality and common development. Politically, China depends on other developing countries, while at the same time it also sticks to the principle of safeguarding their interests. Economically, China is dedicated to realizing common development, and pays much attention to carrying out all-round practical cooperation with other developing countries. Culturally, China emphasizes exchange and mutual learning with other developing countries and endeavors to promote consensus regarding respect for cultural diversity. In terms of security, China sees other developing countries as trustworthy partners for cooperation, and is committed to jointly building a favorable international environment for peaceful development.

1) Equality is the Core Principle in China's Diplomacy with Other Developing Countries

China is the largest and most populous developing country in the world. As a country still on the road to national independence and development, China always regards other developing countries as its companions. Equality is therefore the key characteristic of their partnerships.

Since the founding of the PRC, China has established the core concept of its diplomacy with other developing countries. China holds the view that all countries, large or small, are equal. As early as in 1953, then Chinese Premier Zhou Enlai, introduced the 'Five Principles of Peaceful Coexistence' in his meeting with an Indian delegation. The 'Five Principles' consist of 'respecting each other's sovereignty and territorial integrity, never invading each other, never interfering in each other's domestic affairs, and achieving mutual benefit based on equality and peaceful co-existence'. During his visit to 13 Asian and African countries between 1963 and 1964, Premier Zhou Enlai introduced the 'Eight Principles of China's Economic and Technological Assistance to Foreign Countries' which summarized experiences that China had learned from providing foreign assistance. These principles have been applied in China's assistance to Africa and other developing countries. The Eight Principles include equality, mutual benefit and non-interference in each other's internal affairs, earnestly helping recipient countries to achieve self-reliance, ensuring that recipient countries are the real beneficiaries, alleviating the burdens of recipient countries, and earnestly fulfilling due obligations. The 'Eight Principles of China's Economic and Technological Assistance to Foreign Countries', of which equality, mutual benefit and 'no strings attached' are the core values, have always been the basic principles in China's foreign aid. The principle concept of both the 'Five Principles of Peaceful Coexistence' and the 'Eight Principles in China's Economic and Technological Assistance to Foreign Countries', in the final analysis, is equality, which is still upheld in China's diplomacy today.

In January 1964, Premier Zhou Enlai visited Guinea's cigarette and match factories built with China's assistance

(http://ln.people.com.cn/n/2014/0504/c339837-21126817.html)

    The principle of equality is at the heart of China's fundamental proposition in dealing with relations between countries, and also demonstrates China's determination to safeguard the peaceful development of the international community. Regardless of how the international situation evolves, China always upholds the principle of respecting the rights of other countries to independently implement their own social systems and development paths, as well as the principle of respecting cultural diversity. China believes that all countries, large or small, strong or weak, rich or poor, are equal members of international society and that the internal affairs of a country should be handled by its own people, while international issues should be properly resolved through negotiation among related countries.

    China stands firmly against interfering in the internal affairs of other countries, particularly when large and strong countries interfere or impose on small and weak countries. China itself was once subject to the humiliation of becoming a semi-colonial and semi-feudal society, and was made to sign a series of unequal treaties under the aggression and force of Western powers. These treaties damaged China's sovereignty and territorial integrity, resulting in a divided China. The impacts of this can to some extent still be felt even today. For example, the separation of Taiwan from the mainland and China's territorial disputes with its neighboring countries are inherently linked to that part of Chinese history. It is therefore of great significance for China to strive for national independence and to safeguard sovereignty and integrity. There is an ancient Chinese saying: 'do not do to others what you would not want others to do to you'. China does not welcome any foreign interference in its internal affairs and will not intervene in the internal affairs of any other country. Historically, China has not only learnt to cherish sovereignty and territorial integrity, but also the common aspirations and interests shared by other developing countries in Asia, Africa and Latin America, which were also once subject to colonial rule.

2) Common Development is the Core Objective of China's Diplomacy with Other Developing Countries

From China's perspective, there is only one world which is shared by all countries. To achieve common development is therefore an important foundation of the sustainable development of all humanity which, at the same time, serves the long-term fundamental interests of people all over the world. Development is of even greater strategic importance for developing countries. Without development, they cannot eliminate poverty and backwardness nor achieve lasting peace and stability, let alone provide a happy and stable life for their people. The realization of common development is therefore the core objective of China's diplomacy with other developing countries.

Common development is shared by all people and is based on people's vital interests. Economic globalization should bring universal benefits, especially to the various developing countries, instead of exacerbating the polarization of wealth. China is committed to narrowing the gap between the North and the South by supporting other developing countries to increase their self-reliance, and China sincerely hopes that everyone can enjoy the benefits of development in the 21st century.

Common development is also the foundation of a peaceful world. Many of the problems that developing countries are entangled with, such as poverty, corruption, terrorism, conflict and civil war, are directly or indirectly linked to development. Development is therefore the ultimate solution to the various problems that developing countries face, and resolving these problems through common development is the most effective way to achieve global peace.

II. China's Contribution to South-South Cooperation

China is an active advocate and participant in South-South cooperation. China's contribution to South-South cooperation is mainly manifested in the three aspects of economic cooperation, development assistance and knowledge cooperation.

1) China's Contribution to South-South Economic Cooperation

Based on the principles of equality and mutual benefit, practicality, diversification and common development, China has taken proactive measures to promote South-South economic development and realize common development while at the same time pressing ahead with its own exploration of development. China's major contributions to South-South economic cooperation can be generalized in the following four aspects.

First, China is an important trading and investment partner for other developing countries, and is also one of the most receptive markets for the least developed countries. Take trade, investment and market opening between China and Africa as an example. According to the *White Paper on China-Africa Economic and Trade Cooperation (2013)*, China became Africa's largest trading partner in 2009. Since January 2012, the 30 least developed African countries that established diplomatic relations with China have been granted zero-tariff treatment for 60% of their exports. By the end of 2012, 22 of them had altogether Rmb910 million worth of tariffs exempted, involving US$1.49 billion worth of goods. In view of the data from the *Report on Development of China's Outward Investment & Economic Cooperation (2016)*, by the end of 2015, Chinese enterprises had invested in 51 African countries with the establishment of approximately 3,000 companies, covering 85% of Africa. *The Forum on China-Africa Cooperation Johannesburg Action Plan (2016-2018)* proposes to implement 50 assistance projects to promote trade and support the course of African trade liberalization. The plan also states that China will continue to help African countries improve trade and transportation, increase the added value of products made by African countries, and boost product exports to China.

Second, as the most important driving force for the global economy, China has made tangible contributions to the stability and development of the world and has maintained a favorable international environment for South-South economic cooperation. When the dramatic currency devaluation caused by the Asian financial crisis broke out in neighboring countries and regions in 1997, China succeeded in maintaining the general stability of the Rmb exchange rate, making a key contribution to regional economic stability and development. In the global financial crises since 2008, the vigorous yet stable economic growth of China has also made an important contribution to the stability of the global economy. Through multilateral forums or organizations such as the G20, the UN and the World Bank, China has actively called for global attention on the adverse impacts of the financial crisis on developing countries, in an effort to reduce them. China is committed to supporting the improvement of infrastructure in other developing countries and helping them to boost economic growth. In relation to this, China has taken proactive measures, such as contributing towards the establishment of the Asian Infrastructure Investment Bank (AIIB), the BRICS Development Bank, and the Silk Road Fund.

Third, China has contributed with all its might to the further reform of the global economic governance mechanism, while at the same time safeguarding the interests of developing countries and committing itself to strengthening their voice within the mechanism. China advocates a multilateral trading system which is 'balanced, inclusive and mutually beneficial', and seeks to establish a new international economic and trading order with a higher level of fairness and equality. Through its active involvement in international dialogue and cooperation mechanisms such as the G20 and the BRICS Summit, China has helped to steer the reform of the international financial system in a fairer and more equitable direction. China continues to consolidate its cooperation with emerging countries in the areas of economy, finance, trade and investment, deepening South-South cooperation and taking it to a new level. China has also taken proactive measures to implement the Millennium Development Goals (MDGs), and China is the only country to reduce poverty among its population by half ahead of schedule, making a significant contribution to the MDGs. Regarding the implementation of the UN's 2030 Agenda for Sustainable Development, China is committed to helping other developing countries promote development capacity, optimize the international environment for development, and establish a far-reaching development partnership. China also spares no efforts in pushing South-

South cooperation onto the track of a higher level, a wider scope and a larger scale, strives to discover a route of fair, open, all-round and innovative development which can be shared among developing countries, and advances the common interests of mankind.

Fourth, China has actively pushed forward the cooperation among developing countries in emerging fields. For example, in tackling climate change, China has resolutely fulfilled its international obligations commensurate with its level of development and national strength, and provided necessary financial and technical support to other developing countries in energy conservation, carbon-emission reduction, low-carbon economy development and adaptation to climate change. Since November 2009, China has carried out more than 100 clean energy projects in African countries, including bio-gas technology cooperation with Tunisia, Guinea and Sudan, hydroelectric power generating facilities in Cameroon, Burundi and Guinea, and cooperation in solar and wind power generation in Morocco, Ethiopia and South Africa. China has also donated energy-efficient lamps, air conditioners and other anti-climate change materials to Nigeria, Benin and Madagascar. All of these measures have raised the ability of African countries to adapt to climate change. In the Mekong River Basin, China, Thailand, Cambodia, Laos, Myanmar and Vietnam jointly established the new Lancang-Mekong Cooperation mechanism in 2016. The mechanism promotes risk assessment to detect and release early warning of tropical diseases, boosts cooperation in supervision and maintenance of watershed hydrology, forests and ecology, advances the construction of a spatial information exchange and cooperation center, and facilitates cooperation in emerging areas such as regional information and communication technology and its application training.

2) China's Contribution to South-South Development Assistance

China's assistance to other developing countries is unique in its form and serves as a model for South-South assistance. Most of the assistance provided by Western countries is 'instructional' in nature, while the assistance from China is integrated with cooperation, with the aim of exploring and realizing common development with other developing countries.

The uniqueness of China's assistance to other developing countries lies in both the incorporation of China's own experience of development, as well as the creative and respectful combination of this with the realities of other developing countries. China adheres to the principles of equality, mutual benefit, and ensuring that no political conditions are attached. The means of assistance depends on the interests of the recipient countries, which means that they take various forms, such as capital, technological, material and human resources. The effects of China's assistance are high in efficiency and relatively low in cost, and make a real contribution to local economic and social development. China has received positive feedback from recipient countries.

The strength of China's assistance to other developing countries is based on the aforementioned principles, yet it is also flexible and highly applicable. China always upholds the principle of respecting the will of recipient countries and not setting any political conditions. China respects the right of other countries to independently choose their paths and models of development, allows them to explore and find a development path that best suits their domestic conditions, and never interferes in their internal affairs or pursues political privilege under the pretext of providing assistance. Such practice allows recipient countries to prioritize assistance projects according to their national development goals. Assistance projects are therefore highly targeted. Meanwhile, China's assistance to foreign countries is not invariably the same, but follows the evolution of situations both at home and abroad as well as the development needs of other developing countries. In addition, China attaches great importance to constantly learning from experience and adjusting and updating its forms of foreign assistance, making them highly practical. This assistance model is based on the reality of the recipient countries, making it both flexible and adaptable.

The focus of China's assistance to other developing countries is on infrastructure, agriculture, medical and healthcare, education and other projects relating to quality of life. For developing countries, the main obstacles to development are poor infrastructure and agriculture. Agriculture is the foundation for industrial development and an important prerequisite for the reduction of poverty as it produces abundant labor forces and raw materials for production. Through establishing agricultural technology demonstration centers, dispatching agricultural experts to provide consultations and cooperate on technical issues, and training technical and managerial personnel on agriculture in other developing countries, China has taken proactive efforts to help these countries increase their agricultural productivity so that they can effectively cope with food crises. From 2010 to 2012, China assisted with 49 agricultural projects, dispatched over 1,000 agricultural experts to recipient countries, and provided a great quantity of machinery, improved varieties of grain, fertilizers and other agricultural resources. Poor infrastructure is another major factor impeding the development of other developing countries and is therefore China's focus in its assistance to developing countries. By the end of 2009, China had helped other developing countries build a total of 422 economic infrastructure projects. Public facilities built with aid from China mainly include municipal utilities, civilian buildings, wells for water supply, conference centers, sports venues, cultural venues, and scientific, educational and medical facilities. By the end of 2009, China had helped other developing countries build 687 public facilities of various types. From 2010 to 2012, China assisted 86 construction projects of public cultural venues, sports venues, office buildings and conference centers in other developing countries. The Tanzania-Zambia Railway and the Conference Center of African Union built by China have become monuments of China-Africa friendship.

China has paid constant close attention to providing assistance to other developing countries in the areas of education, healthcare, medical care, emergency humanitarian aid and natural disaster relief. For example, China made great contributions to African countries in their efforts to fight Ebola epidemics in 2014. China was one of the first countries to participate in the prevention and treatment of Ebola and has provided aid materials to Africa. China's total amount of financial aid and assistance far exceeds that of other countries. By November 20, 2014, China had provided the affected countries with four batches of aid worth a total of Rmb750 million (approximately US$120 million), dispatched an accumulation of 450 medical staff to the first front, built mobile bio labs and treatment centers for the affected countries, and helped ten neighboring countries reduce the risk of Ebola importations, so as to push forward the long-term public health cooperation between China and Africa. For another example, in 2011 and 2012, the Horn of Africa and the Sahel were struck by severe drought and over 30 million people were faced with a serious food shortage. In 2011, the Chinese government provided two batches of emergency food aid worth Rmb443 million to countries in the Horn of Africa, such as Ethiopia, Kenya, Djibouti and Somalia. In 2012, the Chinese government provided Rmb70 million worth of emergency food aid to Chad, Mali, Niger and other countries in the Sahel.

In addition, China launched an assistance fund for South-South cooperation in 2016 with an initial pledge of US$2 billion in support of developing countries' implementation of the 2030 agenda for sustainable development. In September 2015 when the UN Sustainable Development Summit was held, President Xi Jinping announced the provision of the '6x100' project support to developing countries in poverty reduction, the agricultural sector and other fields, approximately 300 of which have been implemented.

China's assistance to other developing countries within the framework of South-South cooperation is not limited to material assistance. China's economic growth and its achievement in national construction are both a model and driving force for other developing countries. China's experience in development shows that, through hard work and effort, it is possible for developing countries to find a development path which best suits their domestic conditions.

China's material assistance to African countries in fighting Ebola
(http://news.xsjk.net/jbjkkx/jbrd/20148/367021.html)

3) China's Contribution to South-South Knowledge Cooperation

China is an avid supporter and active participant in South-South knowledge cooperation. On the one hand, China shares its experience and ideas in reform and opening up with other developing countries, supporting them to enhance their capacity for self-reliant development. On the other hand, China also learns from and draws on the merits of the experiences of other countries, in an effort to address the problems of unbalanced, uncoordinated and unsustainable development it has come across.

In recent years, China has developed multi-faceted cooperative knowledge measures in various fields and at various levels with international financial organizations and other developing countries. Since 2008, China and the World Bank have held a series of high-level seminars on 'China-Africa Development Experience Sharing', actively promoting the exchange of experiences of development and policies in various fields such as agriculture, infrastructure construction, economic development zones and other areas between China and African countries. In 2008, China and the Asian Development Bank (ADB) together launched the 'PRC–ADB Knowledge Sharing Platform', oriented towards developing countries in Asia and Africa to promote the exchange of policies and sharing of experiences in the fields of city development, transportation infrastructure, agriculture, and rural development among developing countries in the Asia-Pacific region. This platform is recognized as one of the five successful South-South knowledge cooperation cases in the Asia-pacific region and has been showcased at the Fourth High-Level Forum for Aid Effectiveness (HLF-4) held in Busan. China has also jointly held the 'South-South Knowledge Cooperation Seminar' with the International Fund for Agricultural Development (IFAD) for the fourth consecutive year, helping to promote the exchange of policy and experiences in agriculture and poverty alleviation in developing countries in Asia and Africa. In early 2012, China launched a joint initiative with the ADB called the 'Regional Knowledge Sharing Initiative (RKSI)', which further enhances knowledge cooperation in the Asia-Pacific region. The focus of RKSI is to promote policy dialogue, knowledge exchange and institutional capacity building within the Greater Mekong Sub-Regional Economic Cooperation and Central Asia Regional Economic Cooperation mechanisms. In April 2016, the School of South-South Cooperation and Development was set up at Peking University. As of 2018, more than 50 students from developing countries had studied there.

III. New Progress in China-Africa Relations

China-Africa cooperation is praised as a model for South-South cooperation. Due to its equality, practicality and high efficiency, China-Africa cooperation influences Africa's cooperation with the rest of the world. Currently, China-Africa cooperation continues to grow rapidly both in the areas and extent of cooperation. In the modern era, China-Africa relations have adopted the following five features.

1) China-Africa Relations Have Entered a New Stage of Mechanism Building with the Establishment of the Forum on China-Africa Cooperation (FOCAC)

In 2000, China and African countries jointly set up the Forum on China-Africa Cooperation (FOCAC). Currently, FOCAC has become an effective mechanism to conduct regular collective negotiations, dialogue and practical cooperation between China and African countries. The mechanism is committed to pushing forward China-Africa comprehensive strategic partnership featuring equality and mutual trust in politics, win-win cooperation in the economy, exchanges and mutual learning in culture, mutual defense in security, and unity and cooperation in international affairs. FOCAC is a platform for dialogue between the governments and leaders of both sides on an equal footing. It is also a mechanism that is inclusive of all social sectors such as enterprises, women, media and so on - namely, the Conference of Chinese and African Entrepreneurs, the China-Africa People's Forum, the Forum on China-Africa Media Cooperation, the Africa-China Young Leaders Forum and the FOCAC Media Seminar. The scope of FOCAC has gradually extended from political to economic, cultural, and various social fields, and FOCAC itself has grown from a platform for inter-governmental dialogue to include cooperative dialogue among enterprises, media and NGOs from both sides. This not only meets the needs of further developing China-Africa relations, but is also beneficial to deepening the mutual trust and practical cooperation between both parties. The ever-increasing dialogue mechanisms under the framework of FOCAC send a strong signal to the outside world that China and Africa are deepening their comprehensive strategic partnership, and promoting unity and cooperation between developing countries. FOCAC has the following characteristics. First, it gives great prominence to promoting tangible cooperation, which is embodied in numerous initiatives, projects, follow-up executions and their practical results. For example, the 'Eight Measures' and 'Eight New Measures' pledged by the Chinese government to assist Africa at the 3rd and 4th Ministerial Conferences of the Forum on China-Africa Cooperation. In December 2015, when FOCAC celebrated the 15th anniversary of its founding, President Xi Jinping announced, during his visit to South Africa, ten major cooperation projects covering industrialization, modern agriculture, infrastructure, finance, green development, trade and investment facilitation, poverty reduction and people's welfare, public health, cultural exchange, and peace and security. These projects aim to benefit African people, and have received unanimous support from all African countries. Second, it gives great prominence to African countries' capacity building. China is dedicated to assisting Africa's development, especially in human resources development and training, paying equal attention to the improvement of weak infrastructure, debt relief and investment, and effectively helping African countries expand development capacity. In recent years, the structure of China-Africa cooperation has been transformed and upgraded from general processing trade to capacity cooperation and processing trade, and from project contracting to operation of infrastructure and construction of industrial parks. Third, it gives great prominence to equality and sharing. FOCAC is established on the basis of mutual respect and equal cooperation. The relationship between its participants is not one in which a country (or some countries) teach others, but one that advocates sharing and mutual assistance among peers. Fourth, it gives great prominence to benefiting people. China's efforts to assist Africa's development have been acknowledged by many African countries. FOCAC enables both sides to cooperate more closely in the form of strategic partners to benefit the people of African countries and China.

On November 5, a roundtable of the Beijing Summit of the Forum on China-Africa Cooperation was held in the Great Hall of the People (photograph by Ju Peng, Xinhua News Agency)

2) The Two Issues of China's African Policy Show China Implements a Transparent and Globalized Policy on Africa

On January 12, 2006, China issued *China's African Policy*, which elaborates on the development of China-Africa relations, China's policy on Africa and the overall achievements of China-African cooperation. While reviewing and summarizing the progress and achievements that have been made, this programmatic document also sets the direction and focus of future development and cooperation between the two sides. It is stated in the document that 'sincerity, equality and mutual benefit, solidarity and common development' are the principles of China-Africa exchange and cooperation, and are also the driving force for the continuity of China-Africa relations. China chose to publish the implications of its policy and strategic thinking towards Africa to demonstrate its confidence in managing China-Africa relations and also that China's foreign policy is increasingly transparent and compatible with international norms.

On December 4, 2015, the Chinese government issued in Johannesburg the second *China's African Policy*, which comprehensively expounded the new concepts, proposals and measures of China's policy toward Africa under the new situation. It proposes that China and Africa should make full use of political trust and economic complementarity to promote all-round development of China-Africa cooperation, strengthen South-South cooperation, advance South-North cooperation, and set an example for the establishment of a new type of international relations with win-win cooperation at the core. China upholds an African policy featuring genuineness, tangibility, intimacy and honesty and the correct concept of morality and profit, and promotes friendly and mutually beneficial cooperation between China and Africa to achieve new leapfrog development. Regarding the consolidation of a China-Africa community of shared destiny and the promotion of China-Africa comprehensive development cooperation, the second *China's African Policy* puts forward new measures to further enhance cooperation in seven fields. The document also proposes to further strengthen institutional building of FOCAC, to explore more cooperation fields and new approaches, to promote the establishment and improvement of China-Africa sub-forum mechanisms in the fields of industrialization, modern agriculture, infrastructure construction, human resource development, capacity cooperation, finance, technology, education, culture, health, poverty reduction, legislation among the people of local governments, the youth, women, think tanks and media, so as to deepen the cooperation in relevant areas. Thus, China-Africa cooperation is made more tangible, effective, productive and more beneficial to peoples of China and African countries within the framework of FOCAC.

3) China-Africa Political Cooperation Is Deepening With Continuously Expanding Exchange and Cooperative Measures in the Governance and Security Field

Since the beginning of the 21st century, China and Africa have made positive progress in their efforts to improve diplomacy at governmental, parliamentary, party, public and civil levels, establishing a fully dimensional and multi-faceted system. In the face of new situations at home and abroad, both sides have realized the importance of enhancing cooperation, exchange and mutual learning. Although China and African countries differ from each other in terms of their level of economic development, their histories, cultural traditions and their domestic political systems, they are confronted with similar problems and challenges in their exploration of development paths. Examples of these include eliminating poverty and hunger, resolving the urban slum problem, narrowing the development gap between different regions, improving the structure of national welfare systems, supporting the development of small and medium-size enterprises, and solving the problem of rural development. It is therefore increasingly significant to enhance exchanges and mutual learning in the fields of governance and economic development. To this end, China's National People's Congress (NPC), the parliaments of African countries and the Pan-African Parliament have increased friendly exchanges. The CPC also develops exchanges of various forms with friendly political parties and organizations of African countries to build mutual understanding and trust. Exchanges between local governments of both sides also continue. Both sides aim to facilitate bilateral exchange and cooperation in local development and administration through the establishment of twin provinces/states or sister cities.

Challenges to Africa's peace and security are currently increasing, presenting complicated and varied tasks in the areas of peacekeeping, combating piracy, counter-terrorism, conflict management and post-war reconstruction. For Africa, development and security are two sides of the same coin. Without security, development cannot be realized, and without development security cannot be achieved. Protecting its legitimate rights in Africa from the impacts and threats of terrorism and extremist forces has become a vital part of China's protection of its overseas interests. Enhancing security cooperation between China and Africa is of crucial significance to both sides, and is also a new driving force for China-Africa cooperation. On the one hand, China supports the UN in its resolution of regional conflicts in Africa, actively contributes to UN peacekeeping operations in Africa and is strengthening communication and coordination between China and Africa in the UNSC. On the other hand, China and Africa have been increasing their bilateral and multilateral regional security cooperation. The Fifth Ministerial Conference of FOCAC emphasized the enhancement of security cooperation between China and Africa. The *Beijing Action Plan (2013-2015)* released after the conference reiterates China's commitment to maintaining the peace and stability of Africa together with African governments on the basis of equality and mutual respect. In order to enhance its cooperation with Africa on peace and security issues, China launched the 'Initiative on China-Africa Cooperative Partnership for Peace and Security' and within its capabilities provides financial and technical support to the African Union for its peacekeeping operations and other activities such as the construction of the 'African Peace and Security Framework', personnel exchanges and training in the peace and security field, and prevention, management and the resolution of African conflicts, post-conflict reconstruction and development. In the Johannesburg Summit & the 6th Ministerial Conference Forum on China-Africa Cooperation, security cooperation became one of the five pillars of the China-Africa comprehensive strategic partnership. China supports African countries' efforts to independently solve Africa's problems in an African way. On the basis of fully respecting Africa's wishes, non-interference in Africa's internal affairs and adhering to basic norms governing international relations, China has played a constructive role in promoting peace and security in Africa.

4) China and Africa are on a Path Toward Common Development with Rapid Growth in Economic Cooperation

China has become Africa's largest trade partner, with Africa now being a major importer for China, as well as its second largest overseas construction project contract market and fourth largest investment destination. Economic and trade development between the two countries has improved people's livelihoods, diversified economic development in African countries, provided strong support for China's socio-economic development, and contributed to promoting South-South cooperation and balanced global economic development.

Manufacturing is China's key investment field in Africa. Investments from Chinese enterprises have brought about all-round changes in Africa's social development. Between 2009 and 2012, direct investment from Chinese enterprises into Africa's manufacturing sector totaled US$1.33

billion. By the end of 2012, China's investment in Africa's manufacturing industry had reached US$3.43 billion. Countries such as Ethiopia have attracted a large amount of Chinese investment. Chinese enterprises have set up glass, leather, medical capsule and automobile manufacturing companies in Ethiopia, and invested in textile and steel pipe manufacturing projects in Uganda. These investments have compensated for these countries' unfavorable natural conditions and limited natural resources, increased their tax revenues and employment, and extended the value-added chain of 'made in Africa' products. In Zimbabwe, Chinese enterprises investing in cash crop cultivation have provided interest-free loans to local farmers, improved production infrastructure, offered technical guidance for the whole production process, organized local employees to visit China, and funded local schools and orphanages, all of which have promoted the positive interaction and common development of Chinese enterprises and local society.

China attaches great importance to integrating assistance and technical cooperation, as well as increasing Africa's capacity for economic development. In terms of comparative advantages, Africa's exports are mainly primary products, including energy resources and agricultural products. Technical support and assistance to Africa's energy resource and agricultural industries are therefore priority areas for China's assistance. In terms of agricultural assistance, China continues to emphasize offering technical assistance to African countries and at the same time assisting their agricultural exports to China. Since 2005, China has implemented a zero-tariff policy for some African products. Agricultural products are one of the major beneficiaries of this policy and as a result the export of African agricultural specialties to China has increased rapidly. For example, China's imports of sesame have grown rapidly since it implemented a zero-tariff rate on such products. Sesame imports grew from US$97 million in 2005 to US$441 million in 2011, an annual increase of 28.7%. Chinese agricultural technology and equipment are advanced and practical, low in cost and easy to handle. All of these criteria meet the current general needs of African countries. China's Ministry of Agriculture and Ministry of Science and Technology have provided substantial support to recipient countries in Africa in both non-agricultural industries and technology transfer. The Chinese government has assisted African countries to improve their self-reliance in developing their agricultural industry by providing assistance for the construction of demonstration centers for agricultural technology and sending senior agricultural experts and technicians to teach practical techniques and managerial expertise in agricultural production to the locals. Since 2006, China has helped set up 15 agricultural demonstration centers in Rwanda, the Democratic Republic of Congo and Mozambique, to name a few, and is planning to develop seven more. China has also sent technical groups and several hundred technicians to Africa to provide policy consultation, teach practical techniques and train local staff. Chad has seen its yields grow by over 25% on over 500 hectares planted as a result of China's aid in a project aimed at boosting yield and quality crop varieties which involved training several thousand farmers. Agriculture is the foundation for industrialization: the least developed countries in Africa, particularly the landlocked developing countries which have limited access to resources, have little chance of achieving substantial economic growth without improvements in agriculture. China's agricultural assistance to African countries significantly enhances their capacity for economic development.

4) Regular Cultural Exchanges between China and Africa Boost Friendship and Mutual Trust

There have been increasing cultural exchanges between China and Africa in recent years. These include the Chinese-African Cultures in Focus, the Joint Research and Exchange Plan, the Think Tanks Forum, the People's Forum and the Young Leaders Forum. China and Africa have set up 29 Confucius Institutes or Classrooms in approximately 20 African countries. Every year, the Chinese government provides more than 5,000 scholarships for African countries and trains over 6,000 Africans in various professions. In nearly six years since the Beijing Summit, China and Africa have successfully carried out five series of cultural activities of 'the Chinese/African Cultures in Focus', three 'Visit Programs for African Cultural Personnel' and two 'Exchange Visit Programs for both Chinese and African Cultural Personnel', arranged 43 reciprocal visits of high-level cultural personnel, signed 36 new bilateral government cultural agreements and execution plans, and held approximately 70 exchange performances in African countries (performed 160 times) with the participation of over 1,600 artists from both Chinese and African art troupes. China has also participated in more than 30 art festivals in African countries, organized more than 30 Chinese and African exchange exhibitions, and carried out over 20 cooperative HR training programs, with the participation of more than 160 people from both sides, and covering such areas as state governance, plastic arts, large-scale celebrations, handicraft, choreography and acrobatics. In addition, China has provided cultural material assistance worth Rmb7.2 million to African countries distributed on

36 occasions. The Forum on China-Africa Cooperation Johannesburg Action Plan (2016-2018) issued on December 10, 2015 proposes to invest more to strengthen China-Africa cultural exchange. In addition to supporting existing cultural cooperation projects, China has promised to help build five cultural centers for Africa, intensify African human resource training in the cultural field by establishing ten major 'African Culture Training Bases', and to execute the 'One Thousand People Program' for African culture training.

On November 24, 2007, the First China-Africa Exhibition of Intangible Cultural Heritage was opened in Beijing. Beijing folk artist Xie Lanxiang (right), talks with Zimbabwean folk artists Caroline (middle) and Knight (left) at the World Flowers Exhibition in the Beijing Grand View Garden. (photographed by Zhang Xu, Xinhua News Agency)

Culture is both the adhesive and the lubricant of China-Africa relations. Since the beginning of the 21st century, China-Africa cultural exchanges can be characterized as follows. First, China-Africa cultural exchanges attract a lot of attention and have the full support from the leaders of both sides. Second, the platforms for cultural exchanges have been improved with the creation of new communication brands. A series of brands for communication and cooperation have been launched by the Chinese Ministry of Culture in recent years, including the 'Chinese-African Cultures in Focus', the 'African Cultural Visitors Program', the 'Cultural Policy Roundtable Conference' and the 'China-Africa Visiting Artists' Creative Workshop'. In addition, the Ministry of Culture has further improved the construction and development of China's Art Center in Africa. Third, ideological exchanges are highly emphasized. The cultural authorities of China and African countries pay a lot of attention to ideological communication and dialogue. They aim to boost mutual understanding and learning among people of all social sectors by actively organizing multi-channeled and multi-faceted ideological communication in various fields between governments, civil organizations, cultural personnel and enterprises of both sides. Fourth, much emphasis has been placed on cultural cooperation which benefits the livelihoods of African people. In order to make cultural development beneficial to the vast population of Africa, China strives to integrate cultural and economic developments by doubling its cooperative efforts in the cultural industry with Africa.

In his speech to the parliament of the Republic of the Congo in 2013, Chinese President Xi Jinping strongly emphasized the fact that China-Africa relations are rooted in exchanges between people. Mutual understanding is the key to friendship. The growth of China-Africa relations calls for both 'firm' support for economic and trade cooperation and 'soft' aid through cultural exchanges of people. People-to-people cultural exchanges form an important pillar to maintain this new type of China-Africa partnership. China's former Premier Zhou Enlai once vividly compared a country's diplomacy, economy and culture to an airplane, with diplomacy as the fuselage and economy and culture as the two wings. Propelled by the progression of cultural and economic cooperation, China-Africa relations will fly higher in a broader sky.

To summarize, in its diplomacy with other developing countries, China observes principles and morality, values friendship and seeks justice. China will always be a good friend, brother and partner for other developing countries.

(By Zhang Haibing)

Chapter 5

China's Practice in Multilateral Diplomacy

Since the implementation of the reform and opening-up strategy, China's relations with the rest of the world have undergone historic changes. With the rise of interdependence and co-existence, the world is moving toward 'a Community with a Shared Future for Humanity' where China's identity and role is profoundly changing, so that its future is interconnected with that of other countries. China has become an active participant and advocate of multilateral diplomacy. Multilateralism is a vital concept in China's diplomacy, and multilateral institutions are considered an important means for it to participate in global, regional and territorial governance. With increasing globalization and regionalization, and the emergence of new global problems, multilateral concepts, multilateral institutions and multilateral diplomacy are all subject to change. In playing an active part in the reform and construction of multilateral institutions, China is contributing more new ideas and concepts to the development of multilateralism than ever before.

I. Reasons Why China is an Active Advocate and Practitioner of Multilateral Diplomacy

Since the founding of the PRC, China's attitude toward multilateral international organizations and multilateral diplomacy has significantly changed. Once suspicious and critical of these diplomatic strategies, China began to participate and make use of them, and is now comprehensively integrated into them and makes constructive contributions. The Chinese government first began 'actively participating in various international organizations and actively carrying out multilateral diplomatic activities' in 1986. Since then China has played a proactive and constructive role in multilateral diplomacy, which is now an important feature of China's overall diplomacy. In the report to the 18th CPC National Congress, it was clearly specified that China would actively participate in multilateral affairs, support the UN, the G20, the SCO, BRICS and other multilateral organizations, and play an active role in international affairs, so as to make the international order and system more just and equal. On March 21, 2013, in a telephone conversation with then UN General-Secretary Ban Ki-moon, Chinese President Xi Jinping also emphasized that China will always be a firm supporter and an important partner of the UN, and strongly advocates and practices multilateralism. In January 2017, in a speech at the UN Office in Geneva, President Xi Jinping reiterated that multilateralism is an effective way to maintain peace and promote development, and that "China remains unchanged in its commitment to multilateralism." China's active participation in multilateral diplomacy derives from profound changes in its world outlook, the historic transformation of its international identity and the continued expansion of its national interests.

1) Profound Changes in China's World Outlook

China boasts a rich history and culture. For quite some time, it was at the center of the world and held a sense of cultural superiority. However, in the modern era China was subject to humiliation and subjugation by foreign forces and was removed from the center to the fringes of the world. After the founding of the PRC, the context of confrontation between two superpowers in the Cold War meant that China faced a severe environment and was excluded from the international system. Under such circumstances, while upholding a self-reliant, independent and peaceful diplomacy, China's initial world view was through a prism of war and revolution.

China's world outlook has fundamentally changed since the 1970s. After an accurate judgment and analysis of the evolution of the international situation, Deng Xiaoping pointed out that another world war was not likely to happen in the foreseeable future and that peace and development would continue to be the dominant international relations for a long period, with development being the key issue. Since then, peace and development have become China's basis in judging the international situation. China realizes that its 'future is inextricably linked with that of the rest of the world' and has therefore begun its historical journey of participating in, and integrating into, the world.

With the rise of economic globalization and social informatization since the start of the 21stcentury, China's relations with the rest of the world are undergoing historical changes. The future of China is more closely connected to that of the rest of the world than ever before, and its world outlook has further developed. China's new perspective of the world includes the concepts of a 'global village' and 'a global community with a common destiny', and with these issues in mind China is endeavoring to build a 'harmonious world'.

2) Historic Adjustments to China's International Identity

After the founding of modern China, many attempts were made to participate in multilateral diplomacy and multilateral organizations such as the UN. Due to the objection of some Western countries, however, China was excluded from international organizations for a long time, resulting in China developing a generally negative and critical attitude toward such international organizations. At that time China held the opinion that those international systems were exploitative, unreasonable and unjust, and that China itself should play the role of 'reformer' with the aim of building 'a new world order without imperialism, capitalism and exploitative systems'. China once carried out a 'revolutionized' diplomacy, withdrawing from all international organizations and remaining absent from any international conferences.

Since reform and opening up, China has accelerated its steps towards opening up to the outside world. China's identity in international systems has fundamentally changed from being a 'revolutionary' to being a 'participant' accordingly, and it has started to become more global, adopting a more positive mindset. The report to the 15th National Congress of the CPC introduced the notion that 'China must actively participate in multilateral diplomatic activities and fulfill its role in the UN and other international organizations'. It is on this basis that China is gradually developing a multi-dimensional, multi-leveled and wide-ranging path of opening up.

Upon entering the 21st century, China's role and identity in international systems has transitioned from being a 'participant' to being an 'architect'. China has 'advocated mutually beneficial cooperation, mutual support in difficult times, sharing rights and fulfilling obligations… in order to become more actively involved in international affairs, to adhere to its responsibilities as a major country and to work with other countries to meet global challenges'. China has promoted the idea of building a 'harmonious world', courageously taken up its responsibility as a major country and played a constructive role in the reform and improvement of international systems.

3) The Expansion of China's National Interests

Since reform and opening up, China has been increasingly integrated into the economic globalization agenda and is becoming one of the most progressive and prominent countries in terms of building its national strength. China is also a major power and an engine that drives globalization and the opening up of trade with the constant expansion of its overseas interests. Effectively protecting national interests is the most important objective in the diplomacy of any country. When China's interests grow to the point of exceeding bilateral interests, the most effective way to protect its interests is to conduct multilateral diplomacy, enhancing the multilateral coordination between major countries and giving greater scope to multilateral mechanisms at global, regional and territorial levels, and this will help China better protect its national interests.

On the other hand, as economic globalization and social informatization increase, international relations is reaching a holistic stage of development of interdependence and mutual reliance among different countries and there is an increasing convergence of interests. However, some global problems are becoming more prominent to the point where all countries are affected. As national interests become more interconnected, all countries are confronting an increasing number of disparate challenges. This forces the international community to enhance cooperative measures and improve the efficacy of multilateral mechanisms to resolve all of these problems. China has made it clear that it will 'share opportunities for development and rise to challenges together' with other countries, and that it is 'committed to bringing together the interests of the Chinese people with the interests of people of other countries'. China will continue to contribute to regional and global development through its own development, and expand areas where its interests converge with those of other countries, in order to construct and develop a community of common interests in various fields and at various levels with other countries and regions for the benefit of the common interests of humanity.

4) China has become an Advocate and Practitioner of Multilateral Diplomacy

With the profound transformation of China's perspective of the world, its identity and its interests, China has begun to make proactive efforts to participate in and advocate multilateral diplomacy.

China has continued to participate in multilateral diplomacy since it first adopted it as a diplomatic practice. In 1954, China first attended the Geneva Conference as a major country. In 1955, China attended the Bandung Conference. China also endeavored to restore its legitimate seat in the United Nations and applied for membership of the World Health Organization (WHO), World Meteorological Organization, International Labor Organization (ILO), IMF, World Bank (WB) and other global organizations. China also joined a number of international socialist organizations and institutions led by the former Soviet Union. However, generally speaking, due to the constraints of its standard of living, its exclusion by Western countries and China's ideology, multilateral diplomacy was marginalized in China's diplomatic strategy in this period, remaining subordinate to other policies.

Since the implementation of its reform and opening-up policy, China has gradually developed a new diplomatic strategy of 'non-alignment and not targeting any third party' and has directed more attention to developing normal relations with all countries, based on independence and self-reliance. This adjustment in China's diplomatic strategy has provided a good opportunity for China to implement its multilateral diplomacy. In 1986, China, for the first time, set forth that "it must widely participate in international organizations of various types, and actively carry out multilateral diplomatic activities in an effort to boost cooperation with other countries in every field." Since then, statements in government reports regarding multilateral diplomatic policy have been increasing annually (with the exception of the 1987 report). In the *Report of the 18th National Congress of the CPC* in 1997, it was clearly specified for the first time that China must 'actively participate in multilateral diplomatic activities and fulfill its role in the UN and other international organizations'.

During this period, China began to participate in almost every international organization, so that by 1996, its participation in international organizations had increased to 70% of that of the US, 80% of that of India and 180% of the world's average level of participation. In terms of its participation in global intergovernmental organizations, China reached the level of 90% of that of the US in 1996.[1] China is remarkable not only in its efforts to join international organizations but also in its observance of existing

---

1 A. I. Johnston: *Some Considerations on China's Participation in International Institutions [J]*. World Economics and Politics, 1997, (7) page 7

institutions: 'China is the most well-behaved in observing the rules', and also 'the most virtuous member'. [2] More importantly, China established the SCO and actively participates in this multilateral international organization to resolve hotspot issues, and promotes the formation of a cooperation platform for emerging major countries. These demonstrate that China has become an important and constructive force in promoting the reform of global economic governance mechanisms.

While it continues to open up to the outside world and integrate further into the international community in the 21st century, China also stresses the importance of playing a greater role in multilateral fields and more actively fulfilling its responsibility as a big country. During this process, a new strategic diplomatic structure of 'big countries as the key, neighboring countries as the priority, developing countries as the foundation, and multilateral diplomacy as the stage' has been established. Multilateral diplomacy has become a vital part of China's diplomatic strategy which, as a practice, has made a historic leap from being marginalized to the coordination and overall development of bilateralism and multilateralism.

China's practice of multilateral diplomacy has the following distinctive features. First, it is centered on the UN and upholds the latter's leading role. Second, it prioritizes joining international economic organizations, with the aim of acquiring technological assistance and economic expertise to serve China's economic development. Third, it regards neighboring countries as key, and contributes to the common development and prosperity of the Asia-Pacific region through profound involvement in regional and sub-regional multilateral cooperation mechanisms. Fourth, it is committed to protecting the interests of developing countries and steering the international order in a fairer and more equal direction. Fifth, China actively participates in global governance, strengthens international cooperation and works with the rest of the world to solve global problems and crises.

---

2 E. F. Vogel: *Living with China: US-China Relations in the 21st Century [M].Beijing: Xinhua Publishing House,1998, pages104-105*

The Harmonious World Concept

- China's participation in multilateral diplomacy aims to maintain world peace and promote common development. China advocates, and is committed to, promoting the construction of new international relations with win-win cooperation as its core, and building a human community of shared destiny. China pursues its own peaceful foreign policy. China promotes friendly and cooperative relations with all other countries. It does not form alliances with other countries or groups, nor does it interfere in the internal affairs of other countries. China bases its decision on a particular issue according to its advantages and disadvantages. China plays an active and constructive role in upholding justice in international affairs.

- China aligns its interests with the interests of the rest of the world. It seeks to establish and expand a community of common interests in various fields and at various levels with other countries and regions. China is committed to promoting the common interests of all of humanity.

- China is actively engaged in handling multilateral issues and addressing global issues. In fulfilling its international responsibility, it plays a constructive role in steering the international political and economic order in a fairer and more equal direction. China also promotes democracy in international relations.

- China resolutely safeguards the international order based on the core of the purposes and principles of the UN's Charter, abides by international law and the generally-accepted principles governing international relations, and carries forward the spirit of democracy, harmony, cooperation and sharing in dealing with international relations.

- China advocates a new concept of common, comprehensive, cooperative and sustainable security, and pursues the realization of comprehensive security, common security and cooperative security.

- China promotes regional cooperation and good-neighborly relations. China actively enhances friendly cooperation with its

> *neighbors and works with them to promote a harmonious Asia. China promotes regional economic integration and the improvement of current regional and sub-regional cooperative mechanisms. China is open to alternative proposals for regional cooperation, and welcomes countries outside the region to play a constructive role in promoting regional peace and development.*

The State Council Information Office of the PRC. China's Peaceful Development (White Paper)(http://www.scio.gov.cn)

II. The UN is an Important Platform for China's Multilateral Diplomacy

1) China's Recognition of the UN

For quite a long time after the PRC was founded, China saw the UN as a tool employed by the US and the former Soviet Union in their efforts to seek hegemony. In the early days after the restoration of its legitimate seat in the UN, China's participation in the UN was rather limited, 'highly selective and symbolic' and maintained mostly on the discussion of abstract principles, absent from voting on many issues. In the 158 resolutions of the United Nations Security Council (UNSC) from November 24, 1971 to December 22, 1976, China didn't exercise its right to vote 46 times, ranking the first in all permanent members of the UNSC. After the implementation of the reform and opening-up policy, although China accelerated its steps to integrate into the international system, and gradually joined many specialized agencies and affiliated groups, its contribution to the UN was still limited, lacking in the awareness of setting an agenda and seldom coming up with constructive solutions.

With the deepening of China's reform and opening up, its view of the UN has changed significantly. China has begun to understand the UN's important role in safeguarding world peace and development, its unique yet extensive influence as well as its authority in establishing international order. Guided by the notion of 'taking initiative gradually', China has joined the six principal organs of the UN and other specialized agencies, and participates in all important meetings and activities under the UN framework.

With the rise of globalization and the increasing prominence of global issues since the beginning of the 21st century, China has begun to evaluate the UN in a more active way, and to creatively incorporate the UN into its multilateral strategy. Addressing the UN Millennium Summit in September 2009, then-President of China Jiang Zemin stressed that "the active role of the UN should only be strengthened rather than weakened, and the UN's authority must be upheld rather than challenged". In the *Position Paper of the PRC on UN Reform* issued by the Chinese government in 2005, the UN is regarded as the most universal, representative and authoritative intergovernmental international organization and the best platform to practice multilateralism. China unwaveringly supports the UN's indispensable role in addressing international affairs.

The transition of China's view of the UN has prompted it to actively participate in the UN's activities in a wide range of areas, to advocate, support, and practice multilateralism, and to fulfill its responsibilities as a big country on topics such as UN reforms, security, development and human rights.

2) China is Actively Participating in UN Reforms

In the more than 60 years since its founding, the UN has played an invaluable role in maintaining world peace and promoting human progress and development. However, the UN lags behind in the context of ever increasing global challenges and varied security threats. As a mechanism it is overstaffed and its efficiency is low, while at the same time it is confronted with disputes in almost every field. In light of the new situation of ever prominent global challenges and diversified security threats, the UN is seriously lagging behind in mechanism building, featuring not only overstaffed organizations and low efficiency, but also being confronted with disputes in almost every field. It is widely acknowledged by member states that reform of the UN is imperative. However, big differences remain among member states concerning the focus, specific procedures, and the priority of the reforms. Disagreement is particularly prominent regarding UNSC reform, a key area of the UN reforms. This has resulted in a confrontation between the 'G4 Nations' and 'countries with similar views', covering issues such as the expansion of the UNSC, its seat distribution plan, and the rights members are entitled to.

China has always adopted a positive attitude towards the UN reforms, supporting the UN to keep abreast with the times and conducting necessary and reasonable reforms. China maintains that the aim of the reform is to enhance the UN's role by improving its ability to coordinate national responses to new global threats and challenges. The principle is to adhere to the aims and guidelines of the UN Charter. The method is to conduct the reforms through democratic and thorough consultations and by reaching a general consensus. In this process, priority should be given to increasing the representation and voice of developing countries. China believes that the entire mechanism of the UN must be reformed to address the issue of expanding the UNSC and improving the efficiency and authority of the UN. Therefore it calls for balanced progress in the three major fields of security, development and human rights. On July 9, 2005, the Chinese government issued the *Position Paper of the PRC on UN Reform*, stressing the basic principles for the implementation of UN reform and presenting constructive suggestions to ensure that the reform heads in the right direction.

Since 2005, the UN has adopted a series of reforms and has made some progress, even though the achievements have not met the expectations of some member states.

> **The Position of the Chinese Government on UN Reform**
>
> *China maintains that UN reform should observe the following principles:*
>
> - *Reform should be in the interest of multilateralism and enhance the UN's authority and efficiency, as well as its capacity to deal with new threats and challenges.*
>
> - *Reform should uphold the objectives and principles enshrined in the UN Charter, especially those of sovereign equality, non-interference in internal affairs, peaceful resolution of conflicts and strengthening international cooperation.*
>
> - *Reform should be implemented in all dimensions and areas, and aim to improve both security and development. Reforms should in particular aim at reversing the tendency of the UN to 'prioritize security over development', by increasing inputs in the field of development and facilitating the realization of the MDGs*
>
> - *Reform should accommodate the propositions and concerns of all member states, particularly those of developing countries. Reforms should be based on democratic and thorough consultations and a general consensus.*
>
> - *Reform should proceed from gradually tackling manageable problems to more challenging ones. They must be carried out in a way that will promote and maintain solidarity among member states.*

China stresses that further reforms should be advanced in various fields based on the results that have already been achieved and on democratic and thorough consultations in the international community. In particular, investment in developing areas should be increased so as to deliver great benefits to vast developing countries. China would like to work with other countries to push forward the UNSC reforms onto the track of being conducive to the long-term interests of the UN and to the solidarity among all the member states

3) China's Contribution to the UN Millennium Development Goals (MDGs)

Development is one of the key focuses of the UN, particularly for the majority of developing countries. It covers a wide range of areas and various corresponding challenges, of which the issues of poverty, hunger, disease, education and unemployment are the most prominent. At the UN Millennium Summit held in September 2000, leaders from all over the world promised to deliver on the following eight MDGs: to halve the percentage of global poverty from the 1990 level by the year 2015; to promote elementary education; to promote gender equality; to reduce maternal and child mortality; to tackle the spread of AIDS and malaria; to promote the sustainable development of the environment; and to facilitate global partnerships.

As a developing country, China has made a remarkable contribution to the implementation of the MDGs. China has fulfilled its objectives and made remarkable achievements in the areas of poverty reduction, healthcare and education. Poverty among its population dropped from 689 million in 1990 to 57 million in 2015. China's remarkable achievements in this area, as then UN Secretary-General Ban Ki-moon put it, reduced poverty among the global population by three-quarters.

In addition, China provides assistance to other countries and regions as its capacity permits. By the end of 2009, China had given assistance worth Rmb256.3 billion to 161 countries and over 30 international and regional organizations, reduced or canceled 380 debts incurred by 50 heavily indebted poor countries and least developed countries, trained 120,000 people for other developing countries, and sent a total of 21,000 medical personnel and nearly 10,000 teachers abroad to help other countries. China encourages the least developed countries to expand exports to China and has pledged zero-tariff treatment to over 95% of the exports to China by all the least developed countries which have diplomatic relations with China.

China's experience and contributions are invaluable for the eradication of global poverty, and provide a 'vivid example' of how MDGs can be realized through cooperation within the international community.

4) China's Important Role in Upholding World Peace and Addressing Global Challenges

Peacekeeping operations are a core means of the UNSC to fulfill its obligation in safeguarding world peace and security. It also facilitates the UN in augmenting its authority, giving play to the collective security mechanism, and promoting multilateralism. The first UN peacekeeping mission was launched in 1948. Through continued expansion and development, the responsibilities and scope of peacekeeping operations have rapidly increased, especially in a post-Cold War era of increasing civil war and international conflict. Peacekeeping operations now play an increasingly important role in addressing regional conflicts and maintaining regional peace and stability.

The history of China's involvement in UN peacekeeping operations is relatively short. After its return to the UN, China was once skeptical about and opposed to UN peacekeeping operations. However, since the 1980s, China has changed its approach and gradually become a part of the peacekeeping mechanism. In 1981, the Chinese government made it clear that, in principle, China would support peacekeeping operations which were consistent with the UN Charters. In 1982, it began to pay for its shared cost of peacekeeping operations and became a member of the Special Committee on Peacekeeping Operations. In 1989, China submitted a formal request to the United Nations Truce Supervision Organization (UNTSO) to send five military observers to it. The request was approved and since then China has officially begun to participate in UN peacekeeping operations. The principle guiding China's participation in UN peacekeeping operations is clearly specified. UN peacekeeping operations must strictly adhere to the purposes and principles enshrined in the UN Charters, especially the principles of respecting state sovereignty and non-interference in other countries' internal affairs. UN peacekeeping operations should only be launched after getting the consent of the relevant countries in advance, and should strictly observe neutrality and non-use of force except for the purpose of self-defense. Peaceful means, such as good offices, mediation and negotiation, should be sought to settle disputes rather than use coercive measures. Double standards and military interference under the name of the UN should be prohibited. Any decision on launching UN peacekeeping operations must be based on the principle of practicability and capabilities, and no peacekeeping operations should be launched when conditions are not ripe. A peacekeeping force should not become a party involved in a conflict, otherwise the peacekeeping operation would be deviating from its basic purpose. China actively participates in UN peacekeeping operations based on the above principles, and provides a large amount of political, financial and human resources and equipment support to them, giving full play to its active role and actively contributing to the maintenance of world peace and security.

In 1990, China sent five military observers to UNTSO, becoming the first instance of China's participation in UN peacekeeping operations. In 1992, China sent a unit of personnel on a peacekeeping mission for the first time, dispatching an engineering corps of 400 officers to the UN Transitional Authority in Cambodia (UNTAC). In 2001, it established the Peacekeeping Affairs Office of the Ministry of National Defense of the PRC. It joined the UN Standby Arrangement System in 2002. In 2009, it established the Peacekeeping Center of the Ministry of National Defense of the PRC. By the end of 2012, China had dispatched 22,000 military personnel on 23 UN peacekeeping missions. Among the five permanent members of the UNSC, China contributes the largest number of troops and police. It has also dispatched the highest number of personnel for engineering, transportation and medical support out of all of the 115 contributing countries. China contributes the largest share of UN peacekeeping costs out of all developing countries. China's peacekeeping mission is widely appreciated by the UN and the international community for its high professionalism, efficiency and discipline.[3] The UN's then Secretary-General Ban Ki-moon highly praised China's peacekeeping forces: "they have the ability and the confidence to fulfill any task entrusted by the UN".

Aside from participating in UN peacekeeping operations, China has also supported UN resolutions aimed at reducing piracy by dispatching naval ships to conduct escort operations in the Gulf of Aden and waters off Somalia. By December 2010, the Chinese Navy had dispatched seven sorties comprising 18 ship deployments, 16 helicopters, and 490 Special Operation Force (SOF) soldiers on escort missions. At the same time, China is taking proactive steps to participate in international disaster relief operations and

---

3 Bates Gill & Chin-hao Huang: *China's Expanding Role in Peacekeeping Prospects and Policy Implications*. SIPRI Policy Paper No. 25, Stockholm International Peace Research Institute, November 2009

fulfill international humanitarian obligations. As a country in possession of nuclear weapons, China has always supported the complete prohibition and destruction of nuclear weapons. China actively participates in international efforts in the areas of arms control, disarmament and non-proliferation. It upholds the authoritative role of the UN and other related international organizations and multilateral mechanisms in these areas, and believes that existing multilateral arms control, disarmament and non-proliferation systems should be consolidated and strengthened, that the legitimate and reasonable security concerns of all countries should be respected and accommodated, and that global strategic balance and stability should be maintained.

As a permanent member of the UNSC, China has made significant efforts to participate in the work of the UN in various fields and has greatly contributed in areas such as security, development and human rights. All of these help to build China's image as a large country with a strong sense of responsibility and demonstrate its efforts in participating in and advocating multilateralism.

III. China is an Important Participant in the Reform of Global Economic Governance Mechanisms

1) An Era of Change for Global Economic Governance Mechanisms

The significant development of globalization since the end of the Cold War has not only reshaped the pattern of power in international relations, but has also influenced global economic structures and the legitimacy and efficacy of global economic governance mechanisms. The root cause for this phenomenon is the continuous growth in the strength of emerging markets. In particular, with the increasingly leading role of emerging market countries led by the expanding BRICS, the center of global production has been radically relocated. Contrary to this, a proper balance between the transition of economic power and that of the inherent rights and obligations has not been achieved in the global economic system. The impact of the global financial crisis in 2008 and the resulting European sovereign debt crisis further highlighted this contradiction, revealing the failures of the previous economic governance mechanism. This prompted a series of profound changes to the global economic governance mechanism. In this new context, the G20 has gradually become the new platform for international economic cooperation.

The G20 is an informal dialogue mechanism established for developed countries and emerging markets under the framework of the Bretton Woods international financial system, and came into being following the 1997 Asian financial crisis. The mechanism was developed by Western countries with the aim of preventing the recurrence of such a crisis. After the outbreak of the global financial crisis in 2008, the G20 mechanism was transformed into a summit where the leaders of major developed economies and developing countries could discuss crisis response and the coordination of economic and financial policies. The remit of the G20 now covers more areas to reflect the demands of the time and the changes in international powers, signaling that power in terms of global economic governance has shifted from the grasp of developed countries alone to come under the joint management of both developed and developing countries.

The G20 was founded in 1999. When the global financial crisis broke out in 2008, the G20 mechanism was upgraded to a leadership level, and became a mechanism for major developed countries and emerging market economies to negotiate how to deal with the crisis and coordinate economic and financial policies. Since then, the G20 has taken on many brand-new connotations reflecting the demands of the times and objective and realistic changes in international powers. It marked the transformation of global economic governance from developed countries dominance to the joint dominance of both developed and developing countries. In September 2009, the G20 Pittsburgh Summit developed it into a major forum for international economic cooperation.

2) The G20 is the Primary Platform for China's Participation in Global Economic Governance

China is both a founding member and an active participant in the G20 Summit. Hu Jintao, the former Chinese President, attended the first seven G20 Summits, and delivered important speeches in each meeting expounding China's propositions on global economic governance.

In September 2013, President Xi Jinping attended the Eighth G20 Leaders' Summit held in St. Petersburg, Russia, and delivered an important speech, stressing that G20 members should firmly maintain and develop an open world economy, build a closer economic partnership, raise the awareness of forging a community with a shared future for humanity, cooperate in competition and achieve win-win results in cooperation. This visit presented 'China's propositions' and disseminated 'China's voice', which was highly recognized by G20 leaders and widely approved by the international community. From 2014 to 2017, President Xi Jinping attended G20 Leaders' Summits successively and delivered important speeches, making new contributions to leading the development and cooperation of the G20, promoting world economic growth, and improving global economic and financial governance.

In September 2016, the 11th G20 Leaders' Summit held in Hangzhou demonstrated China's deep participation in and its guidance to global economic governance. China as the host country strengthened communication with other G20 members and took the initiative by setting the agenda for issues to be discussed. Making 'Building an Innovative, Invigorated, Interconnected and Inclusive World Economy' the theme of the Summit, China designed four key topics, namely, 'innovation in growth models', 'more efficient global economic and financial governance', 'robust international trade and investment', and 'inclusive and interconnected development'. President Xi Jinping delivered the keynote speech entitled *A New Starting Point for China's Development, A New Blueprint for Global Growth* at the opening ceremony of the G20 Summit, and fully interpreted China's view on global economic governance. Under China's active promotion and guidance, the Summit produced a series of innovative, leading and institutional achievements, and issued the G20 Leaders' Communique Hangzhou Summit and 28 Outcome Documents. The Summit marks a milestone in the history of the G20.

China's Proposals for Enhancing Global Economic Governance

Economic globalization is the irreversible development trend of the times. Meanwhile, we are still faced with multiple risks and challenges. Currently, protectionism is rising; global trade and investment are sluggish; the multilateral trading regime faces bottlenecks in development, and the emergence of various regional trade arrangements has led to fragmentation of rules. Complex geopolitical factors and regional hot-spot issues as well as global challenges are on the rise.

We should enhance macro-economic policy coordination, join forces to promote global economic growth, and help maintain financial stability.

We should strive to expand overall global demand, improve the quality of supply in all respects, and consolidate the foundation of economic growth.

We should innovate new development models, tap growth impetus, adjust policy thinking, and place equal emphasis on short, medium and long-term policies, as well as on demand-side management and supply-side reform.

We should improve global economic governance, solidify its mechanism guarantee, optimize the governance structure of international financial institutions, improve the Global Financial Safety Net, and enhance cooperation in financial oversight, international taxation, and anti-corruption so as to increase the capability of the world economy to resist risks.

We need to build an open world economy, continue to push trade and investment liberalization and facilitation, resolutely avoid beggar-thy-neighbor policies, advocate and promote an open world economy, stay committed to the promise of not adopting new protectionist measures, strengthen coordination and cooperation in investment policies, and take effective action to promote trade growth.

We need to build an interconnected world economy, forge interactive synergy, and realize coordinated development.

We need to build an inclusive world economy to strengthen the foundation for win-win outcomes. We need to eradicate poverty and starvation, advance inclusive and sustainable development, and put the issue of development at the core of the global macro policy framework.

3) China's Contributions to the Reform of Global Economic Governance Mechanisms

China takes the G20 as a key mechanism and platform for its participation in global economic governance. Chinese presidents have attended all of the G20 Leaders' Summits and delivered important speeches, putting forward a series of suggestions and propositions for the G20 mechanism reform and development. China has driven the G20 to transform itself from a mechanism of crisis response to one of long-term governance, making creative contributions to strengthening cooperation among G20 members, promoting global economic growth, and improving global economic governance, fully demonstrating China's identity and role as a contributor and builder in the reform of the global economic governance mechanism.

China advocates that we need to make an effort to build up the G20 and steer the world economy in a sound direction of prosperity and stability. In terms of the G20 mechanism construction, China proposes that the G20, advancing with the times and giving full play to its leading role, should demonstrate a strategic vision, chart a course, and identify a development path for the world economy. The G20 should follow the principle that words should be matched with action. We should make "the G20 an action team instead of a talking club", and implement every action in earnest. The G20 should make joint efforts for the benefit of all involved. We should listen attentively to the voices of countries all around the world, particularly those of the developing countries, so that the G20 will be even more inclusive in its work. It should possess the partnership spirit and realize common development via collaboration.

China proposes to advance the building of an open and free global trading institution and opposes all forms of protectionism, conforming to the historical trend of globalization. China insists that we should increase the representation and voice of developing countries, expressing the aspiration of developing countries. It benefits not only the development of the emerging economies, but also the stability and prosperity of the world economy. In particular, China holds that the international community should enhance assistance to developing countries, and link it with the UN MDGs, safeguarding the interests of many developing countries. With China's advocation and active involvement, the G20 has reached agreement on multiple issues, such as improving the representation of emerging economies and developing countries, and providing more emergency food supplies and agricultural assistance to Africa. China has actively pushed forward cooperation in energy, anti-corruption and climate change, proposed to develop the Belt and Road Initiative into the most extensive international cooperation platform conforming to the trend of economic globalization, advocated building a community with a shared future for humanity, and offered 'China's solution' to address global economic challenges. China is not only an advocate of global economic governance, but also an active practitioner. It has contributed more than 30% to world economic growth for years, becoming a major stabilizer and driver of global economic growth.

The G20 provides a rare opportunity for developing China to participate on an equal footing in global economic governance. Meanwhile, it is another important platform for China to participate in the reform of the global economic governance mechanism and to uphold multilateralism.

IV. China is an Active Participant in Addressing Global Climate Change

1) China is One of the Countries Suffering Most from the Adverse Effects of Climate Change

Nowadays, climate change is the most prominent global environmental problem endangering us all, and also one of the biggest global challenges confronting the international community.

China is one of the most susceptible countries to the adverse effects of climate change. The average temperature of the earth's surface in China increased by 1.1degC between 1908 and 2007, and the warming of China's climate will continue to intensify. Climate change leads to the frequent occurrence of extreme weather events, such as uneven distribution of precipitation, increased likelihood of drought and acceleration of already rising sea levels. In particular, climate change significantly impacts agriculture, livestock farming, forestry, natural ecosystems, water resources, and coastal zones. Since 2011, China has faced a string of extreme weather and climate disasters, including hailstones and snow in the south of China, spring and summer droughts in the middle and lower reaches of the Yangtze river, rainstorms and floods in the south, typhoons in coastal areas, autumn rains in western China, serious water logging in Beijing, and other disasters caused by extreme weather. These weather and climate disasters have significantly impacted China's economic and social development, as well as property and the wellbeing of the population.

While suffering from the huge impacts of climate change, China is under pressure from Western media that depict China as 'the largest carbon dioxide emitter in the world' and as a climate change 'trouble maker'. In fact, China's total carbon dioxide emissions in the past and per capita emissions were lower than those of some developed counties. In more than 50 years from 1950 to 2002, China's carbon dioxide emissions from the burning of fossil fuel accounted for only 9.33% of the world's cumulative emissions. The per capita carbon emissions of China are also far lower than those of the US and Australia.

In terms of the accumulation of greenhouse gas emissions since the Industrial Revolution (1850-2004), China's historical contribution only accounted for 10.8% of the total of the 13 G8+5 countries, and was approximately a quarter of that of the US. China's historically accumulated contribution rate per capita is only 1%, far below the levels of developed countries such as 21.3% for the US, 16% for Canada, 16.4% for the UK, and only higher than India's rate of 0.4%. Moreover, as a major manufacturing country and the largest exporter in the world, China bears a considerable amount of carbon emissions for the benefit of other countries, with 20% to 30% of total carbon emissions responsible for producing goods and offering services for the US, Europe and other countries. This is, in essence, a transfer of carbon dioxide emissions from Western countries to China. In light of the facts, China's responsibility for incurring climate change should be measured in a more objective way.

2) China's Concepts and Suggestions for Addressing Climate Change

Over the past 10 years of rapid economic growth, China has become the world's second largest economy and has become the world's largest emitter of greenhouse gases. China attaches great importance to the issue of climate change. In the report of the 15th National Congress of the CPC, the huge pressure imposed on resources and the environment by population growth and economic development was first brought to attention. In the report to the 16th National Congress of the CPC, it was declared that coordination between economic development, population, resources and the environment should be achieved. In the report to the 17th National Congress of the CPC, the concept of ecological civilization was put forward for the first time, and while giving prominence to this concept, the report to the 18th National Congress of the CPC declared that efforts should be made to build 'a beautiful China'. In the third plenary session of the 18th CPC central committee held in November 2013, it was explicitly stated that the reform of the ecological civilization system should be deepened to accelerate its construction so as to protect the ecological environment by the application of such a system and to promote the establishment of a new modernization pattern for the harmonious development of humans and nature. The report to the 19th CPC National Congress called on people of all countries to work together to build 'a clean and beautiful world'.

In addressing climate change, the Chinese government has taken an active part in global climate governance and has put forward a series of new concepts and suggestions for global governance. The Chinese government advocates building a community with a shared future for humanity, vigorously carries out climate diplomacy, promotes North-South and South-South cooperation, takes the initiative to shoulder the responsibilities of a big country, and adopts effective emission reduction actions. The Chinese government has also adopted multiple proactive measures, including building mechanisms, making laws and regulations, formulating action plans and generating social publicity, and strengthening the top-level design and public awareness of scientific knowledge on addressing climate change, so as to encourage the whole society to widely participate in this campaign and constantly enhance the capability of coping with climate change, thus making great contributions to global climate governance.

China's Concepts and Suggestions for Addressing Climate Change

- *To actively address climate change, strive to control greenhouse gas emissions, improve the national ability to adapt to climate change, and ensure China's economy, energy, ecology, and food security as well as people's lives and property security.*

- *To deeply participate in global governance, build a human community with a shared destiny, and promote the common development of all mankind.*

- *To adhere to the principles of 'common but differentiated responsibilities', fairness, and respective capabilities, promote the effective implementation of the developed countries in taking a lead in substantial reduction of emissions, and providing developing countries with funding, technology and the convention obligations to support capacity building, so as to strive for a fair opportunity of sustainable development for developing countries, and more funds, technology and capacity building support for them, thus promoting North-South cooperation.*

- *To take the initiative to shoulder international obligations according to national conditions, development stages and practical capabilities, and to continuously intensify actions to mitigate emissions and adapt to climate change, and intensify South-South cooperation in addressing climate change.*

- *To extensively carry out international dialogue and exchanges on climate change, strengthen policy coordination and pragmatic*

> *cooperation in relevant fields, share useful experiences and practices, promote climate-friendly technologies, and work with all parties to build a better home for mankind.*

Source: The Information Office of the State Council of the PRC. Strengthened Actions to Tackle Climate Change - China's Independent Contributions. http://www.scio.gov.cn/xwfbh/xwbfbh/wqfbh/2015/20151119/xgbd33811/Document/1455864/1455864.htm. (Log on time:2017-03-30)

3) China is an Active Participant in Addressing Climate Change

China is the first developing country to formulate and implement a National Plan for Coping with Climate Change, and also one of the countries which has made the strongest efforts to save energy and reduce emissions, and taken the fastest pace in the research and development of new and renewable energy in recent years. As early as in 2006, China set an obligatory target of reducing energy consumption by about 20% per unit of GDP by the end of 2010 on the basis of the 2005 level. In 2009, China again promised to cut carbon dioxide emissions by 40% to 45% per unit of GDP by 2020 based on the 2005 level, to make about 15% of non-fossil fuel energy in the primary energy consumption, and increase forest areas by 40 million hectares thereby increasing forest reserves to 1 billion cubic meters from 300 million cubic meters in 2005. During the 11th Five-Year Plan Period, China's energy consumption per unit of GDP was reduced by 19.1%. By 2011, China's energy intensity had been reduced by 2.1%, and by 2012, its carbon intensity had been reduced by more than 3.5%. By 2014, China's carbon dioxide emissions per unit of GDP had fallen by 33.8% compared with 2005. In the *China-US Joint Statement on Climate Change* issued in 2014, China made its first official pledge to endeavor for carbon dioxide emissions to peak around 2030 or earlier and increase the share of non-fossil fuels in primary energy consumption to around 20% by 2030. China has become the world's largest country in energy-saving and in utilization of new energy and renewable energy. In June 2015, China submitted the *Strengthened Actions to Tackle Climate Change - China's Independent Contributions*, in which China proposed its action targets for climate change from 2020 to 2030, implementation plans and policy measures.

China has also played a more constructive role in international negotiations on climate change. Since the official launch of such negotiations in 1990, China has been actively involved in the negotiations and implementation of the convention. As a responsible major country, China not only participated in the *Kyoto Protocol*, demonstrating its political determination to reduce emissions, but has been actively stepping up efforts to reduce emissions. China adheres to the international climate system within the basic framework of the UNFCCC and the *Kyoto Protocol*, plays an active role in the main channel of international climate change negotiations within the UN framework, upholds the principles of fairness, 'common but differentiated responsibilities' and affordability, addresses the issue of climate change within the framework of sustainable development, abides by the principles of openness and transparency, extensive participation, signatory-parties-led and consensus through consultation, actively participates in negotiations, strengthens communication and exchanges among the various parties, and promotes international negotiations on climate change to achieve positive results, thus promoting positive progress in international climate change negotiations.

On November 30, 2015, President Xi Jinping attended the opening activities of the Paris Climate Change Conference, where he delivered an important speech entitled *Working Together to Build a Fair and Reasonable Governance Mechanism of Win-win Cooperation on Climate Change*. He clearly put forward a global governance concept of "doing one's best to obtain win-win results", "upholding the rule of law to achieve fairness and justice", and "practicing tolerance and mutual learning to seek common development". At the same time, he advocated the idea of harmony but not sameness, allowing countries to find countermeasures most suitable for their own national conditions. Therefore, China has formed the concept of global climate governance with its distinctive characteristics. During the Paris Climate Change Conference, the Chinese delegation, with a responsible and constructive attitude, fully participated in all talks, carried out intensive shuttle diplomacy, supported and cooperated with the host country of France and the UN to do a good job in the related aspects, and made outstanding contributions to reaching the Paris Agreement.

China also actively provides public products in the field of climate governance, vigorously promotes South-South cooperation, and tries its best to help developing countries to cope with climate change. As to the problems that many developing countries are confronted with, such as poor infrastructure, vulnerability to the adverse effects of climate change and weak capacity to deal with climate change, China has, for years, provided active support for African countries, small island states and the least developed countries to improve their abilities to address climate change. Since 2011,

China has invested Rmb410 million to help dozens of countries to improve their infrastructure for climate change, and enhance their capacity-building to address climate change. In September 2015, China announced that it would set up a China Fund for South-South Cooperation on Climate Change, and would launch such cooperative programs as 10 low-carbon emission demonstration areas, 100 projects to mitigate and adapt to climate change, and training programs for 1,000 people to address climate change in developing countries starting from 2016.

Climate change is a global problem. China has demonstrated its determination to actively respond to climate change, and brought hope and confidence to the global campaign of addressing climate change through its declaration to endeavor to build 'a beautiful China', incorporate ecological civilization construction into the whole process of economic, political, cultural and social construction, and realize the sustainable development of the Chinese nation. Guided by the concept of innovative, coordinated, green, open and shared development, China will make greater contributions to addressing global climate change and building a 'clean and beautiful' world, and will become an important participant, contributor and leader in the construction of global ecological civilization.

(By Zhang Pei)

Chapter 6

How China Conducts Public Diplomacy

The Chinese government values both its official relationships with foreign governments and interactions with different social sectors and people in other countries. Guided by the strategy of soft power, the Chinese government emphasizes the significance of promoting Chinese culture through public diplomacy as an important part of China's overall diplomacy. China's public diplomacy shares common characteristics with that of other countries and also displays its own uniqueness, constituting its own concepts and features and confronting its own difficulties and challenges. The success of China's diplomacy would not be possible without the promotion of public diplomacy.

I. Reasons for China to Carry out Public Diplomacy During Recent Years

For the past few years, China has particularly emphasized the significance of public diplomacy due to internal and external factors, specifically due to its own rapid development and the world's growing demand for China.

1) Public Diplomacy is the Fundamental Requirement for Upholding Peaceful Development and Building a Community with a Shared Future for Humanity

(1) Developing the Soft Power of Culture and Shouldering the Responsibilities as a Major World Power

Since the reform and opening up more than 30 years ago, China has made great progress in its comprehensive national strength and has increased its influence in the world. It is widely acknowledged among foreign experts that the 2008 Beijing Olympic Games and 2010 Shanghai World EXPO, which were the first events of their kind to be held in a major developing country, signified that China was becoming a major world power. As China moves ever closer to the center of the world stage, President Xi Jinping points out that China will shoulder more international responsibilities and obligations to the best of its ability and make greater contributions to the peaceful development of mankind[1]. President Xi Jinping has reiterated that friendship, which derives from close contacts between peoples, holds the key to sound state-to-state relations. China must call for the participation of the vast majority if it wants to make greater contributions to the peaceful development of mankind. The spiritual communication and intimacy between peoples are the foundation of national diplomacy. This raises new demands for public diplomacy.

On the evening of August 8, 2008, the grand opening ceremony of the 29th Beijing Olympic Games was held at the National Stadium. This is the fireworks show at the opening ceremony. (photographed by Chen Kai, Xinhua News Agency)

In 2007, the Chinese government stressed the importance of the development and prosperity of Chinese culture domestically and building China's soft power through promoting its culture and public diplomacy in foreign affairs, in order to enhance China's political influence, economic competitiveness, and moral appeal with an amiable presence in the world.

---

1. Xi Jinping: *Unswervingly Stick to the Road of Peaceful Development, Resolutely Strive for World Peace and Development*. March 19th, 2013. (The report's Chinese version is available at: http://cpc.people.com.cn/n/2013/0320/c64094-20845746)

In 1990, American professor Joseph Nye introduced the idea that soft power is not a carrot or stick, but rather an ability to attract and influence other countries, to the point that even those countries which initially resist that influence ultimately have no choice but to follow due to the power of the trend. China advocates the construction of the spiritual and ideological attraction different from hard power, and proposes a new public diplomacy concept unlike that of western countries.

China boasts a long standing history of civilization and splendid cultural resources. The improvement of social civilization and people's education level is conducive to increasing China's attractiveness, thus improving its influence and image in the international community. The power of culture differs from military conquest or economic competitiveness. It is a silent, transformative influence that can influence people through affinity. China pursues an independent peaceful foreign policy, implements a mutual benefit and win-win strategy that is more in line with the interests of China and the rest of the world, strengthens domestic and foreign two-way cultural exchanges, and solidifies the construction of the national cultural soft power. What China has done in this regard is widely welcomed all over the world, and improves its international image.

On October 10, 2010, tourists at the Shanghai World Expo Park queued up around the Poland Pavilion waiting for a visit. (photographed by Xu Jinquan, Xinhua News Agency)

(2) Improving People's International Consciousness to Support China's Foreign Policies

Along with the process of modernization, the thoughts and ideas of the Chinese people are increasingly diversified, especially after the information revolution, which has introduced new technology like computers, mobile phones, and the internet into people's daily life. As there are more than 750 million netizens in China at present, the general public now has more opportunities and platforms to express their opinions on both the country's domestic and foreign policies. Therefore, China's public diplomacy is not only oriented towards foreign societies and peoples, but also oriented towards the Chinese masses and professionals from all walks of life. Due to its comparatively low level of modernization, China is unable to completely satisfy its diplomatic need as a big country with its unique features. Therefore, it is a hot debate among the general public, especially among the netizens, as to why China should take the path of peaceful development, why China should provide international communities with more public products, and why China should aid other developing countries. The implementation of public diplomacy can help guide people to rationally look at the relationship between China and the outside world and form a correct view of national interests, so as to let them understand and support the Chinese government's foreign policies.

2) Public Diplomacy is a Necessity for China to Cope with Outside Questioning and Make Greater Contributions to the World

(1) Dealing with and Debunking the 'China threat argument'

Since 1978 when the policy of reform and opening up to the outside world was implemented, China has adopted an omnidirectional foreign policy, striving to create and maintain a peaceful and stable international environment, a good-neighborly environment, an equal and mutually beneficial environment for cooperation and an objective and friendly environment for public opinion. Meanwhile, as China rises, there is a lot of news about the 'China collapse theory', 'China threat theory' and 'China contending for hegemony' in the world, which implies that people in some countries still harbor suspicion and distrust of China. For example, China's cooperative projects in Africa are framed as 'new colonialism' and 'new energy colonialism', and China's international cultural exchanges are described as 'cultural invasion' and 'brainwashing tactics'. Since western media has a loud voice in international communication, it impacts the attitude of people all over the world.

(2) Reducing Misunderstanding to Improve Mutual Trust

When colonizing Asia, Africa and America, Western powers not only occupied lands and markets with warships and commodities, but also captured people with religion and culture, ruined the local history and civilization, altered the local languages and words, and inseminated the 'centrism of Western culture'. Despite the national independence of most colonies after the Second World War, it is still very difficult to eliminate the impact of western ideology and culture. So far, Western countries have always been the preferred destinations for elites and young people from developing countries to pursue their overseas education, and they are also the first choice of travel destinations for middle-income tourists from developing countries. The majority of popular media, advertising, television shows and films are imported from Western countries. As there is a severe lack of communication and exchanges among developing countries, it's no wonder why people from other countries are short of knowledge about Chinese society and people, and harbor misunderstandings about us.

China has been enjoying its unique culture and tradition, has adopted a socialist system different from western countries, and now is undergoing great changes, making it difficult for foreign social elites and the general public to understand it. For example, most ethnic groups in the world have a certain religion. There is no dominant religion for the Han nationality which constitutes over 90% of China's total population, and of which the patriarchal clan is the foundation of the society and its people are enlightened through moral education. Moreover, unlike the multi-party systems, separation of powers and democratic elections of Western societies, China's socialist political system was created out of revolution and improved under the leadership of the CPC, and is therefore a unique system. As a major emerging country, China has experienced great changes over the past six decades, spanning more than 40 years since its reform and opening up, which has astonished many foreigners who knew China well before. They realize that they need to learn about China again.

(3) Contributing to Global Cultural Exchange

Against the background of globalization, there appears to be an increase in the level of interdependence among people in different countries. Without understanding, support and cooperation among people in different countries, global economic, political and security cooperation would be impossible. Support from people both in China and the rest of the world is therefore the most solid foundation for the success of China's diplomacy.

The integration and competition of different cultures in the world is accelerated by globalization, giving rise to many new phenomena. First, for centuries in modern history, cultures had been transmitted in one direction, from western culture to non-western ones only. Nevertheless, nowadays we have witnessed an increase in bi-directional or multi-directional cultural communication. Second, globalization and modernization have, on the one hand, given rise to a homogeneity of industrial civilization and popular culture. At the same time, they have allowed all nationalities to become aware of the value of their own cultures and to preserve them as a result. Last, the multicultural values advocated by the UN have won support across the world and constitute a consensus among different peoples. No culture is either superior nor inferior to another, and every culture can and should make greater contributions to human progress. This requires China and other developing countries to adapt their cultures in the global transition toward social modernization and to communicate actively in the international community to enrich human civilization.

In this context, the Chinese government, social elites and the general public have developed a great passion for enhancing the soft power of Chinese culture and developing public diplomacy. Countries all over the world appreciate China's development of its soft power, and are gaining a deeper understanding of China through its public diplomacy.

II. The Principles Underpinning China's Development of Public Diplomacy

China shares many similar ideas to other countries concerning public diplomacy. For example, they may agree that public diplomacy must mobilize officials, social elites and the general public to communicate with foreign government officials, and more directly with foreign social elites and ordinary people. This enables the general public of other countries to acquire a clearer understanding of their national policy, adopt a more positive attitude towards their country and influence the policies of their own governments towards their country. China is no exception in this regard. However, in view of its own conditions and difficulties, the Chinese government particularly highlights the following ideas.

1) Telling True Stories about the Real China

Only a small number of people in the world have been able to come and visit China, while the vast majority can only learn about China through indirect channels such as media. Even those who have visited might not acquire an accurate, comprehensive and thorough understanding of such a vast and complicated country within a limited period of time, not to mention those who haven't been there. Therefore, China should showcase and explain Chinese culture to the world via public diplomacy and help them understand us better. The Chinese prefer a sincere attitude, namely communication on an equal footing rather than being condescending, and to convince by reason rather than coercion. The people of China want to show the world the real China, not some unreal fantasy focused solely on its positive points without flaws. Propaganda and false images of China only produces adverse effects and reduces credibility, and therefore China criticizes and discredits malicious propaganda while presenting the facts to speak the truth, since facts speak louder than words and give lies nowhere to breed. China will win the sympathy and support of the majority of people through genuineness and sincerity.

China has gradually expanded and strengthened its direct communications with foreign governments and societies. These dialogues have become more frequent with China's opening up to the outside world, and have also been supported by the world's understanding and acceptance of China. Through its policy of 'non-interference in the internal affairs of other countries', China generally only kept in contact with foreign ruling parties and the social organizations that supported them in the past. However, many countries have lots of political parties, and their distinctive parties and social organizations greatly influence the diplomatic policies of their governments. Accordingly, China's public diplomacy must keep up with the times, and the Chinese government has therefore begun to communicate with various parties and social organizations and to deepen its bilateral and multilateral relations with other countries. For example, the CPC not only communicates with communist, socialist and other left-wing political parties, but also contacts different political parties and organizations, which has been rewarding. On the other hand, these political parties and social organizations are willing to learn about China and have interacted with the Chinese government and people more actively and frequently.

2) Mutual Learning, Understanding and Communication

China's public diplomacy also enables it to learn from and adopt advanced ideas, experiences and practices of other countries. Although in recent years, some intellectuals in Western countries have repeatedly suggested that there is much to learn from the emerging and developing countries, their public diplomacy has not included any elements from the cultures of other nationalities due to their sense of superiority, namely 'Western cultural centralism'.

China's public diplomacy emphasizes treating other countries as equals and advocates learning from them to mend its own weak points. The Chinese have always held the idea that in order to achieve progress, they have to embrace diversity and stay modest and prudent. As a developing country, China must also draw on achievements across humanity to achieve its own success. In the past, China mainly followed the path of developed Western countries, but now values the experiences and lessons to be learned from all countries. The CPC aims to make China a study-oriented country, with a study-oriented Chinese society. China welcomes all friendly advice, dialogue and constructive criticism.

3) Transcending Differences in Social System and Ideology

Since the cold war, the influence of ideological barriers and the cold war mentality have not been eradicated. Since the reform and opening up, the Chinese government has exerted great efforts to transcend the differences in social system and ideology in its public diplomacy so as to make new friends and make as many of them as possible, search for similarities and common points in ideas and thoughts, and seek common ground while putting aside differences, thus laying a solid supportive foundation for China's foreign policies. For example, Robert A. Scalapino, a celebrated professor at the University of California - Berkeley, was misguided by his anti-communist thinking early in his academic career. However, after Nixon's official visit to China in 1972, Scalapino visited China many times and engaged in deep discussions with Chinese academics and scholars, allowing him to adopt a more objective and pragmatic view about China. Finally, he served as chairman of the National Committee on US-China Relations, and interviewed and sponsored many young and middle-aged Chinese people to go to America as visiting scholars in order to develop their research, which also resulted in the corresponding development of China-US relations. At the same time, he expressed many rational ideas which helped to improve the relationship and US policies towards China. In his biography *From Leavenworth to Lhasa*, he regarded his research on China as a significant achievement of his life's work and his trip to the Roof of the World as an honor. Many other foreign elites and leaders have also changed their rigid and outdated impressions of China after visiting and studying its way of life. China firmly resists 'brainwashing tactics' in terms of its public diplomacy and is willing to help foreign elites and people to understand China. China believes that foreign governments and people can seek common ground while setting aside their differences and establish friendly and cooperative relationships with China.

4) Respecting the Reality of Global Diversity

Many nations gained independence from their colonizers after the Second World War. Through the advocacy of the UN and the joint efforts of different countries in the world, respect for cultural diversity has become the mainstream in the international community. Like many other emerging countries, China values its own sovereignty, respects the sovereignty of others and maintains its right to choose its own path of development. The Chinese people recognize that the history, culture and national conditions can vary from country to country, so they must get to know and understand others and hence respect the choices made by their people.

With increasing interdependence as a result of globalization, different countries have to reach a basic consensus on many issues to further promote global cooperation. China determines its decision or stance on a particular issue according to its benefits and costs so as to uphold integrity, fight for justice, make policies and take action. For example, many foreign governments and people denounce policies of discrimination against African Americans in the US and the segregation policies in South Africa. The Chinese government and people also regard these policies as violations of the spirit of the UN Charter and publicly denounce them. On issues which are very complicated or subtle and where consensus is difficult to reach, China demonstrates an attitude of constructive involvement through its public diplomacy. With the keen consideration of the real interests of the parties involved, China's diplomacy in general, as well as its public diplomacy, operate on the belief that people in the country concerned should define their own destinies, for external efforts produce only limited effects, and China would never act as a 'backseat driver'. China stands firmly against military interference, regime change and jeopardizing property and the safety of civilians. China also opposes the pursuit of hegemony and power under the guise of maintaining justice.

III. New Practices and Characteristics of China's Public Diplomacy

Since the beginning of the 21st century, China has made some rewarding explorations in its public diplomacy. Since 2007, China's public diplomacy has come under the spotlight with its new practices and characteristics.

Chapter 6

1) The Public Diplomacy of Leaders and Government Officials: Authoritative and Affinitive

Since the year 2000, Chinese leaders and government officials have become involved in more diplomatic activities, developing relations with top foreign government officials while also promoting public diplomacy in various forms. Their behavior is, to a large extent, reflected in the country's image, and has a great influence on the public at home and abroad.

Ambassador Fu Ying, chairwoman of the foreign affairs committee of the 12th National People's Congress and former vice foreign minister, has made fruitful efforts in public diplomacy. She once delivered speeches at Eton College and Oxford University when she served as ambassador to the United Kingdom, where both teachers and students asserted that China had grown to be a world power and worried that China would impose its will on others as China grew stronger. Fu Ying said it was true that China's GDP had surpassed the UK but that the UK's per capita GDP was 15 times higher than China's. The area and population of the UK was almost the same as one of China's provinces, Hunan Province, but its GDP was 17 times as much as that of Hunan. The UK was in a post-industrial society and its urban residents comprised 90% of the population, while in China, 60% were rural residents. Even the number of disabled people in China exceeded the total population of the UK. Therefore, China's strength was quantitative and incremental, while its weakness was in per capita and qualitative measurements. Fu Ying's analysis was convincing. Not only did she directly address the public in foreign countries, but she also made China's voice heard by taking full advantage of general media, getting articles published in newspapers and engaging in dialogue and debate on TV. In April 2008 when the Beijing Olympic torch was relayed in London, in response to the negative coverage of the British media, Fu Ying had an article published in the *Sunday Telegraph*, which sparked a debate in Britain. Many people wrote to support Fu Ying and her article was also reprinted in African newspapers.

Zhao Qizheng, the former Director of the State Council Information Office of the PRC, promotes the idea of 'introducing the real China to the world', and also engages in substantial public diplomatic activities. In his meeting with the heads of *The New York Times* in 2011, he said that the more sensitive a question is, the more necessary it is to answer it. Zhao Qizheng engaged in many candid conversations on the sensitive topic of religion with Lewis Belau, a famous American theologian and religious leader. This led to the co-publication of *Riverside Talks: A Friendly Dialogue between an*

Atheist and a Christian in both Chinese and English. Zhao Qizheng's public diplomacy has changed the impression among foreigners of inflexible Chinese leaders and government officials, and has demonstrated China's perspective and approach as a result of its reform and opening up.

2) Non-governmental Organizations: Civil and Professional

With economic growth, China's middle-income group continues to expand, and the autonomy of social communities and mass organizations is growing higher. According to the *2016 Statistical Bulletin on Social Services Development* issued by the Ministry of Civil Affairs, by the end of 2016, the number of social organizations registered in accordance with the law, namely non-governmental organizations (NGOs), reached 702,000 nationwide, an increase of 6% over the previous year. Some of them have taken an active part in and played their due roles in public diplomacy. For example, the Association of China's Public Diplomacy, established in December 2012, has played the role of a public channel by providing professional services of consultation, coordination and international exchanges. Since its establishment, the association has absorbed many members from government offices, factories, schools, and private enterprises, held lectures, exhibitions and symposiums on China's diplomacy and Chinese culture, and organized activities such as exchange visits by people from the media and social sectors, youths, experts and scholars both at home and abroad, thus making their contribution to the promotion of the development of China's public diplomacy. Of course, China's NGOs are not comparable with China's international status and influence, as they are not active enough nor well known to others, and their participation in international activities and international organizations still remains low.

Among NGOs, think tanks are playing an increasingly important role in public diplomacy. It was explicitly stated in the Third Plenary Session of the 18th National Congress of the CPC held in November 2013 that China should strengthen "building new types of think tanks with Chinese characteristics and improving the decision-making consulting mechanism". With their expertise and experiences of dialogue with foreign dignitaries and elites, the scholars and experts in Chinese think tanks have put forward their analyses on growing world trends and China's domestic and foreign policy-making. These analyses, which are insightful and of strong theoretical significance, have stirred reflections and improvements of policies in China as well as in other countries, and promoted the development of China's bilateral and multilateral relations. At a time when summits and meetings between senior officials of both China-Africa and China-Arab Forums were being convened, dialogue was also held between think tanks, providing policy-makers with much advice. On some sensitive issues, the experts and scholars from think tanks on both sides hold second-track dialogues to explore policy options, so as to provide reference for government departments. For example, although the Taiwan issue, a significant problem faced by China, is China's domestic affair, it is complicated by international factors. The Shanghai Institute for International Studies (SIIS) held several second-track dialogues on the topics of the 'China-EU relationship and the Taiwan issue', the 'China-Japan relationship and the Taiwan issue', and the 'China-ASEAN relationship and the Taiwan issue', which have played a very important role in making different countries understand Cross-Strait relations.

Through various means such as speeches, media interviews and forums, the experts and scholars in think tanks have direct talks with the general public from foreign countries, and they are greatly welcomed for their objective stances and expertise as well as for their not being government officials.

3) People-to-People Cooperation and Communications among Youngsters: Fundamental and Sustainable

The world is now in urgent need of people with Chinese-language proficiency to communicate extensively with China on economics and trade, and to receive more Chinese tourists. Despite their popularity in some prestigious foreign universities, the general lack of Chinese-language courses means that the global need for Chinese-language workers remains unsatisfied. To meet such a demand abroad, the Chinese government established the first Confucius Institute in Seoul, the Republic of Korea in 2004, and provided standard and authoritative textbooks of modern Chinese to teach Chinese to local people in their universities. As of December 31, 2016, China had founded 512 Confucius Institutes and 1,073 Confucius Classrooms in 140 countries, and trained over 1.9 million students. At the same time, China has accumulated substantial experience in the methods of education and ways of running the institutes. A great number of people who have learned Chinese have now joined different social sectors and made contributions to strengthening the cooperation between China and their countries.

In its cooperation with other countries, the Chinese government emphasizes interaction between young people. Within cultural cooperation programs, a certain quota will be reserved every year for cultivating young foreign elites, inviting them to China to participate in research on different topics and projects, and in discussions, studies, and visits with Chinese students to increase their mutual understanding and friendship. Confucius Institutes and exchange programs for young people are important efforts in China's public diplomacy. Looking to the future, China is endeavoring to make more and more friends in the generations to come.

4) Various Cultural and Sports Activities: Recreational and Participatory

As mentioned above, China has hosted grand international events such as the Beijing Olympic Games and the Shanghai World EXPO, and has also hosted a number of large international events in many cities, such as the Xi'an Flower EXPO and the Guangzhou Asian Games. Billions of people across the world watched the opening ceremony of the Beijing Olympic Games and praised its beautiful and exciting presentation of Chinese culture using state-of-the-art technology. Various kinds of cultural and sports events held in China have not only attracted thousands of Chinese tourists, but have also become reasons for foreign tourists and business people to visit China. These events have also significantly improved China's image. For example, the Xi'an Flower EXPO enabled tourists from both China and abroad to learn more about the more recently developed western part of China.

These cultural events are also held in other countries to increase involvement and allow foreign people to learn about Chinese culture while enjoying themselves. In recent years, China has held a 'Chinese Culture Year' and 'Chinese Culture Week' in different parts of the world, which exemplify Chinese culture in the form of exhibitions, shows, publications, film and TV shows in order to narrow the gap between Chinese and foreign people. On April 3, 2012, the first premieres of the China-Korea Friendship Year of People-To-People Exchange, held in Korea, showed artists from both China and Korea starring in the famous Korean drama *Chun Xiang*. The drama features three different aspects of world intangible cultural heritage: the first part was performed in Pingtan (storytelling and ballad singing in Suzhou dialect) and Shaoxing Opera, the second part was by Pansori (a Korean genre of musical storytelling with a vocalist and a drummer), and the last part, *The Wedding of Chun Xiang and Meng Long*, was jointly performed by Chinese and Korean artists. When the curtain fell, the audience broke into rapturous applause. The mainstream media in Korea widely reported the successful opening ceremony, adding to the vivid atmosphere of the event. From September 26, 2011 to January 9, 2012, the Palace Museum of China and Le Louvre Museum of France jointly held an exhibition of French and

Chinese relics dating back to the same historical period in *The Forbidden City at the Louvre - the Chinese Emperors and the French Kings*, leaving visitors with a brand new impression of charming contrasts. Some visitors noted that the development of China and France was synchronized during the Chinese Ming and Qing dynasties, until China isolated itself from the rest of the world, causing it to lag behind. China hopes that Europeans understand its need to develop quickly since its reform and opening up. The exhibition drew much praise from the media and attracted some 140,000 or more visitors.

5) Improvement of China's Media: Extensive and Rapid

In today's world, the influence of the media is ubiquitous and cannot be overlooked. China's public diplomacy is now making improvements in media (including new media) to make the circulation of China's stories more extensive, rapid, influential and effective. Media groups in China have invested substantially in improving hardware so as to satisfy the increasing need of the public to know more about China. More importantly, media software should be improved at the same time, which means that efforts should be taken to make China's stories more well received by foreign audiences.

Therefore, the central and local government departments in China have established a spokesperson mechanism, where government officials participate in interviews and answer questions from journalists, to change their image of indifference towards the media. Domestic and foreign journalists have praised the fact that Chinese ministers present themselves and take questions at televised press conferences, which is quite rare even in Germany.

Emergencies are the best test for the public diplomacy of a country. In spite of various difficulties and risks, Chinese journalists traveled to the affected areas immediately after the 2008 Wenchuan earthquake to make up-to-date, transparent and accurate reports, covering the disaster and rescue work and conveying moving stories to the rest of the world. Presenting the facts also prevented rumors from spreading.

Diplomatic activities via the internet are called 'network public diplomacy', the participants of which are mainly active Chinese and foreign netizens, and through them, network public diplomacy is extended to every corner of society. The websites of the Foreign Ministry and foreign embassies of China are rich in content, and many Chinese embassy websites are ranked among the best in those countries. China has foreign-language websites in more than 60 languages, including the websites set up by local governments mainly in English, and those run by the border provinces in languages of the neighboring countries. More than 700 million Chinese netizens have interacted on the internet with the rest of the world through their own blogs and micro-blogs in a more natural and amiable way than through government websites. They take different perspectives in their observations and analyses, and express the views and opinions of the people. The network, however, is a double-edged sword, and has brought many unprecedented challenges as well. For example, inflammatory information on networks can raise people's anger into mass events. Terrorists, separatists and extremists take advantage of networks to invoke people's hatred and instigate riots and violence. Some countries and forces use networks to interfere with the internal affairs of other countries. Moreover, networks bring hidden risks in information security. For example, 'WikiLeaks' in 2010. Therefore, like other governments, the Chinese government is speeding up the construction of network security, and self-discipline among netizens and the network industry. At the same time, it is carrying out extensive international cooperation to crack down on transnational network crimes.

> **The 'WikiLeaks' Incident (zh.wikipedia.org)**
>
> *In November 28, 2010, through major publications, the website 'WikiLeaks' publicized over 250,000 telegrams sent to the State Council of the United States from more than 250 American embassies. The telegrams were mainly about the countries of residence and contained a lot of critical opinions of some foreign politicians. As a result, the founder of the website Julian Assange is being hunted by the American government and remains in hiding at the Ecuadorean Embassy in the UK.*

IV. Challenges of China's Public Diplomacy

China's public diplomacy has brought great progress as well as new challenges. As China's public diplomacy is still in its initial stage, it will take some time for the Chinese government and people to overcome difficulties and barriers, solve challenges, and summarize their experiences and lessons to improve their public diplomacy. The main challenges of China's public diplomacy are as follows.

1) China's Relatively Low Level of Internationalization

A country's level of internationalization is related to its openness. With half of its population living in rural areas and its relatively low level of comprehensive education and international awareness, China is still in the process of modernization and urbanization. Public diplomacy relies on the cooperation between governments and the people. Thus, the general public are seen as the country's civil ambassadors and as an important component of the national image. Among the 122 million outbound Chinese tourists in 2016, there were people who did boldly what is righteous and saved their compatriots in danger, but there were still some who did not behave in a civil manner nor observe local rules and regulations, leaving a negative impression of China on foreigners.

Today, nationalism, populism and extremism run rampant in the world, and they have had an impact on some ordinary people in China, constituting their particular features. In spite of China's rapid economic growth and improving international status, many Chinese people have not yet mentally adapted to the changes or prepared themselves to become members of a responsible major country. The hundred years of humiliation make it hard for many Chinese people to rid themselves of a sense of inferiority and they are therefore prone to feeling victimized by other countries and overreacting when facing challenges. However, the feeling of inferiority is sometimes turned into self-conceit, and people with few achievements can look down upon others and refuse to learn from them. In spite of their limited representativeness, some self-proclaimed spokespersons of the Chinese people attract attention from the outside world, and are mistakenly viewed as being representative of all Chinese people. Extremism leads some people to become irrational, challenge the rule of law and even resort to violence, all of which exert a negative influence on China's public diplomacy. Due to China's economic development, the middle class has significantly increased, and the autonomy of social communities and organizations continues to be promoted. In Shanghai alone, there are nearly 20,000 highly active NGOs, some of which have begun to expand globally. For example, a rehabilitation club organized by cancer victims in Shanghai has encouraged many cancer patients and others to adopt more positive and optimistic attitudes towards the illness and has now become world famous. However, to match China's identity as a major responsible country, these NGOs must improve their levels of participation in international organizations and activities.

2) 'Demonization' by Some Western Media and Powers

Western countries and media outlets inevitably still have a dominant voice in the international community. For example, Hollywood films account for over 40% of the market share and most information on the internet is written in English and is from developed Western countries. Besides, CNN and BBC news programs are most frequently seen on the television in people's everyday life. Some governments and media in western countries take advantage of this to publicize comments on, and criticism of, developing countries, and even to make them do what they are not willing to, which is totally disapproved of by the elites and people in many developing countries. China is most often 'demonized' by some Western media and powers because it has adopted a socialist system, and made significant economic development and social progress without following Western models. They persist in disseminating the 'Chinese collapse argument' and the 'China threat argument'. As Chinese companies began developing their businesses in Africa, they were promptly labeled as 'neocolonialists' and 'energy resource colonialists'. When the Chinese government and people fight back against separatism and terrorism, they are accused of 'violating human rights'. Although they are criticized by people with global insight their accusations are still misleading and influence the public. When the Chinese government, media and people act to confront these issues, they often feel passive. In order to counter these demonizing accusations, China's public diplomacy must become more proactive and effective so that China's voice is heard and its good intentions of peaceful development are felt by more people in the world.

3) Vicious Distortion of China's Values

Cultural misunderstanding can easily be reduced through cross-cultural communication and mutual understanding. Some Western forces and media, however, have viciously distorted the image of Chinese culture and its core values, resulting in the reluctance of foreign people to visit China. They intentionally shape public opinion by suggesting that Chinese cultural values are different from the cultural values of other countries, which is far from the truth. China's core values, as explicitly stated in the report to the 18th National Congress of the CPC include 'promoting prosperity, democracy, civility, and harmony, upholding freedom, equality, justice and the rule of law', and 'advocating patriotism, dedication, integrity, and friendship'. 'Promoting prosperity, democracy, civility, and harmony' are national values as well as the aims and ideals of nation-building. 'Upholding freedom, equality, justice and the rule of law' are social values which should be realized through the implementation of the country's political, economic and social policies. 'Advocating patriotism, dedication, integrity, and friendship' are individual values. The Chinese government has advocated and cultivated these core values and called for the joint efforts of the whole of society in order to achieve them. In terms of cultural values, China has much in common with other countries in the world, such as peace, development, cooperation and civilization. On the other hand, China has accepted many Western values such as democracy, freedom, equality and the rule of law. The values of human rights have already been written into the *Constitution of the PRC* and progress has been made in the implementation of human rights. China also promotes its own cultural values such as 'harmony', 'integrity', and 'friendship'. China shares common interests with other countries such as the global economy, and also shares much in terms of modernized cultural values, so cooperation and mutual understanding will surely be enhanced.

China acknowledges the contribution that Western culture has made to the world and draws on all refined foreign cultural achievements. However, it does not appreciate the sanctification of 'universal values', and stands firmly against the imposition of this formulaic ideology on others. China supports the idea of cultural diversity promoted by the UN, which acknowledges that every culture has the right to contribute its refined cultural values to global cultural diversity. Through the integration of refined cultural values, countries all over the world may reach a consensus with mutual understanding. The wider and deeper the level of understanding, the stronger will be the solid ideological foundation for a global community with a shared future.

(By Yu Xintian)

Chapter Follow-up Questions and References

Chapter 1

Questions

1. Why is China's path of peaceful development 'a serious choice and a solemn promise made by the Chinese government and people'?
2. How does China's diplomacy allow it to safeguard its national interest on the one hand and to promote the establishment of a harmonious world on the other?
3. What are the main objectives, approaches, conditions and constraints of China's diplomatic strategies?

References

1. Huang Renwei, *Time and Space of China's Rise* [M], Shanghai: Shanghai Academy of Social Sciences Press, 2002
2. Yang Jiemian et al, *The CPC and Diplomatic Theory and Practice with Chinese Characteristics* [M], Shanghai: Oriental Publishing Center, 2011
3. Yang Jiemian et al, *Institutional Restructuring and Standard Rebuilding* [M], Shanghai: Shanghai People's Publishing House, 2012
4. Henry Kissinger, *On China*. NY: New York, The Penguin Press, 2011

Chapter 2

Questions

1. What are the diplomatic concepts, principles and policy proposals that China has developed towards its neighboring countries in terms of the economy, security and military affairs?

2. What is meant by the basic components of 'hiding one's capacities and biding one's time'?

References

1. Deng Xiaoping, *Selected Works of Deng Xiaoping* [M], People's Publishing House, 1993
2. Yang Gongsu & Zhang Zhirong, *Diplomatic Theories and Practices of Contemporary China* [M], Beijing: Peking University Press, 2009
3. A. Acharya, *The Making of Southeast Asia, International Relations of a Region*, Singapore: ISEAS Publishing, 2012

Chapter 3

Questions

1. What are the new concepts, principles and policy ideas that China has adopted in order to cope with relations with other big countries?
2. Why has China proposed building a new type of big country relationship with the United States?
3. How does China perceive emerging powers and cooperate with them?

References

1. Department of Policy Planning, Ministry of Foreign Affairs, PRC (ed), *China's Foreign Affairs* [M], Beijing: World Affairs Press, 2002-2012
2. Qin Yaqing (ed), *Great Power Relations and China's Diplomacy* [M], Beijing: World Affairs Press, 2011
3. Wang Yizhou & Tan Xiuying (ed), *Sixty Years of China's Foreign Affairs (1949-2009)*, Beijing: China Social Sciences Press, 2009
4. David Shambaugh (ed), *Tangled Titans: The United States and China*, Rowman & Littlefield Publishers, Inc, 2013

Chapter 4

Questions

1. What are the principal concepts of China's diplomacy with other developing countries?
2. What are the key factors in China's efforts to maintain friendly relations with African countries?

3. In your opinion, are there any shortcomings in China's diplomacy with other developing countries?

References

1. The government of the PRC, *China's African Policy* [M], January 12, 2006
2. The State Council Information Office of the PRC, *China-Africa Economic and Trade Cooperation* [M], August 29, 2013
3. The State Council Information Office of the PRC, *China's Foreign Aid*, July 10, 2014
4. Zhang Haibing, *Development-Guided Aid: Study on the Model of China's Aid to Africa* [M], Shanghai: Shanghai People's Publishing House, 2013
5. Deborah Brautigam, *The Dragon's Gift: The Real Story of China in Africa*, OUP Oxford, 2009

Chapter 5

Questions

1. Why does China actively participate in multilateral organizations and engage in multilateral diplomatic practice?
2. What contributions has China made to the development of the UN and peace-keeping operations?
3. What is your understanding of China's status quo as a major carbon emitter and its multilateral diplomacy in terms of the environment?

References

1. Qin Yaqing et al, *The International System and China's Diplomacy* [M], Beijing: World Knowledge Press, 2009
2. Wang Yizhou (ed), *Construction in Contradiction – Multiple Insights into the Relationship between China and Key International Organizations* [M], Beijing: China Development Press, 2003
3. Yang Jiexian et al, *The Communist Party of China and Diplomatic Theory and Practice with Chinese Characteristics* [M], Shanghai: Oriental Publishing Center, 2011
4. Zhao Jinjun (ed), *China's Diplomacy 1949-2009* [M], Beijing: Peking University Press, 2010

Chapter 6

Questions

1. What are the characteristics of China's public diplomacy?
2. What are China's methods of conducting public diplomacy?
3. Analyze and compare China's values with the West's 'universal values'.

References

1. Zhao Qizheng, *Public Diplomacy and Cross-Cultural Communication* [M], Beijing: China Renmin University Press, 2011
2. Zhao Qizheng et al, *Cross-Border Dialogues: the Wisdom of Public Diplomacy* [M], Beijing: New World Press, 2012
3. Qiu Yuanping, *China's Peaceful Development and Public Diplomacy* [J], International Studies, 2010, (6)
4. Yu Xintian, *Reflections upon Constructing the Theory of China's Public Diplomacy* [J], International Studies, 2010, (6)
5. Luis Palau & Zhao Qizheng, *Riverside Talks, A friendly Dialogue Between an Atheist and a Christian*, New World Press, 2006